Makhan's PZ Legacy

Mayar Akash

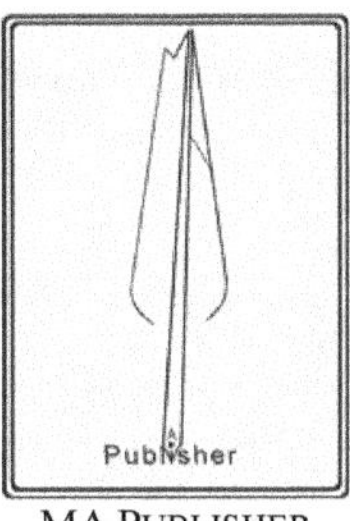

MA PUBLISHER

Produced by MAPublisher for Penny Authors
Email: Pennyauthors@gmail.com
www.pennyauthors.org.uk

Published by MA Publishing (Penzance)
14 Adelaide Street, Penzance, TR18 2ER, Cornwall, England, UK
Email: mapublisher@yahoo.com
www.mapublisher.org.uk

Printed in the region the books have been published: Australia | Canada | Europe | UK | USA

ISBN-13: 9781915958358

Cover designed by Mayar Akash
Cover photo supplied by family
Typeset in Times Roman
Title in Elephant

Paper printed on is FSC Certified, lead free, acid free, buffered paper made from wood-based pulp. Our paper meets the ISO 9706 standard for permanent paper. As such, paper will last several hundred years when stored.

Acknowledgements

This book could not have been written without the generosity, memory, and trust of the people of Penzance and Newlyn. To everyone who shared a story, corrected a detail, posted a photograph, or simply wrote "I remember…" — thank you. Your voices are the foundation of this work, and your willingness to look back with honesty and affection made this project possible.

A special acknowledgement must go to the members of Nostalgic Penzance and Newlyn, a private community of more than 23,400 people, whose shared memories, comments, and conversations helped bring this story to life. Many of the recollections that shaped this book came from that group — from people who took the time to contribute their experiences, identify places, recall names, and keep the past alive through collective memory. Your participation has been invaluable, and this book stands as a testament to the power of community storytelling.

My deepest gratitude goes to the **Dass family**, whose history, resilience, and quiet warmth shaped the social life of this town for more than four decades. Thank you for allowing your story to be held, examined, and celebrated with the care it deserves. This book is written with profound respect for your legacy.

To the former staff of the café, the Riviera Hotel, and Mac's Bar — thank you for sharing the behind-the-scenes stories that brought these places to life. Your memories illuminate the labour, camaraderie, and humour that sustained the family's work.

To the musicians, dancers, and night-owls who kept the soundtrack of Penzance alive — your recollections helped rebuild the rhythm of an era.

To the local historians, archivists, and memory-keepers who preserve the fragments of our shared past — thank you for your diligence, your curiosity, and your commitment to community heritage.

To the friends and readers who encouraged this project from its earliest stages — your belief in the value of everyday history sustained me through the long process of gathering, sorting, and shaping these memories into a coherent whole.

Finally, to the town of Penzance — thank you for holding this story for so long, and for allowing it to be told. This book is a testament to the power of ordinary places, the endurance of community memory, and the quiet beauty of lives lived side by side.

Foreword

There are stories that belong to individuals, and there are stories that belong to communities.

The story of Dass's Café belongs to all of us.

For decades, I have listened to people in Penzance speak about the café with a kind of warmth usually reserved for family. They remember the jukebox, the windows, the laughter, the friendships, the music — but above all, they remember the feeling of being young in a place that welcomed them without judgement.

What strikes me most is how often these memories surface unprompted.
Mention the café in conversation, and faces light up.
People who have not seen each other in years suddenly share the same smile.
It is as if the café still exists, not on Market Jew Street, but in the shared emotional landscape of the town.

This book captures that landscape with extraordinary care.

It honours the Dass family — pioneers of multicultural life in Cornwall — and it honours the hundreds of people whose memories form the backbone of this work. It is rare to see a local history project of such scale, depth, and dignity. Rarer still is a book that manages to be both academically rigorous and profoundly human.

Dass's Café was never just a café.
It was a meeting place, a rite of passage, a cultural crossroads, and a quiet revolution in a town that was changing faster than anyone realised.

This book ensures that the story will not be forgotten.

Preface

How this book came to be

This book began with a single question: *How does a place that no longer exists continue to live so vividly in the memories of a town?*

The answer arrived slowly, through hundreds of voices, fragments, and recollections shared across a decade of online conversations. What started as a casual curiosity became a vast, unexpected archive — 281 memories from more than 175 people, each offering a small window into a world that had quietly slipped into the past.

Dass's Café was not a grand institution. It was not a landmark in the architectural sense. It was a modest café on Market Jew Street, run by a family who worked hard, raised their children, and opened their doors to a generation of young people who were discovering music, independence, and themselves.

And yet, the café became something extraordinary.

As the memories accumulated, a pattern emerged: people were not simply remembering a place. They were remembering a feeling — of belonging, of youth, of possibility. They were remembering the glow of a jukebox, the warmth of a family who welcomed them, the thrill of a song played too loudly, the friendships formed in the windows overlooking the street.

This book is an attempt to honour those memories.
It is built on the voices of the community, shaped by the stories they chose to share, and grounded in the dignity of a family whose presence helped define the social life of Penzance for four decades.

It is not a biography, nor a nostalgic scrapbook, nor a simple local history.
It is all of these things and something more: a testament to the quiet power of everyday places, and to the people who keep them alive long after the doors have closed.

— *Mayar Akash*

Prologue

The glow of a jukebox on Market Jew Street

Imagine Market Jew Street in the late 1950s.

The evening is settling in. Shop shutters are half-down, the pavements still warm from the day. A group of teenagers drifts toward a café halfway down the hill — laughing, jostling, full of the restless energy of youth. They push open the door, and the familiar sound greets them before they even step inside.

A warm hum.
A soft click.
A burst of music.

The jukebox glows in the corner — chrome, colour, and light — casting reflections across the tables. Someone has already fed it a coin. Someone else is arguing about which song should be next. The air smells faintly of coffee, chips from across the street, and the warm valves of the machine.

Behind the counter, Mr Dass looks up with a half-smile — the kind that says he has seen all of this before and still enjoys it. His children weave in and out of the café, part of the scene and yet slightly apart from it, growing up in a world where their home and the town's social life are one and the same.

Outside, the street is dimming.
Inside, the café is alive.

A girl sits in the window, pretending not to notice the boy who keeps glancing her way. A group of lads crowd around the jukebox, arguing about Cliff Richard versus the Everly Brothers. Someone lights a cigarette. Someone else laughs too loudly. Someone is about to fall in love for the first time.

This is not a grand moment in history.
It is an ordinary evening in an ordinary café.

And yet, decades later, people will remember it with a clarity that surprises them. They will remember the music, the warmth, the friendships, the feeling of being young in a world that was just beginning to open up.

They will remember Dass's Café.

And they will remember the family who made it possible.

This book begins here — in the glow of a jukebox, in the hum of a small café, in the memories of a town that still carries the echo of those nights.

Content

Introduction

Why this story matters

Every town has places that shape its identity.
Some are grand — churches, monuments, civic buildings.
Others are small, ordinary, almost invisible to outsiders.

Dass's Café was one of those places.

It was a modest café on Market Jew Street, run by a family whose roots stretched from Bengal to Cornwall. It had chrome tables, a warm jukebox, and a steady stream of teenagers who treated it as their second home. It was a place where friendships formed, romances began, and the soundtrack of a generation played on repeat.

This book tells the story of that café — and the family who made it possible.

It draws on:

- 281 community memories
- 175+ individual voices
- decades of lived experience
- archival fragments
- local music history
- migration narratives
- the geography of Penzance

The aim is not nostalgia for its own sake.
It is to understand how ordinary places become extraordinary through the lives lived within them.

Dass's Café is a lens through which we can explore:

- youth culture in postwar Britain
- early multicultural life in rural Cornwall
- the power of music to shape identity
- the role of small businesses in community life
- the emotional weight of memory
- the quiet dignity of a family who built a home in a new land

This book is not only about the past.
It is about how the past continues to shape the present — in the stories we tell, the places we remember, and the ways we understand ourselves.

Part I — Roots & Arrival

Chapter 1 — A Town on the Edge of Change

Penzance in the 1940s–50s: the world before Dass's Café

Introduction: A Town Between Worlds

Before the jukebox lit up Market Jew Street, before teenagers crowded into chrome-edged booths, before the Dass family became woven into the town's memory, Penzance was a place caught between two eras.

The Second World War had ended, but its shadows lingered.
Ration books were still tucked into kitchen drawers.
Families were rebuilding their lives with quiet determination.
The town's rhythms were familiar, steady, and deeply local.

And yet, beneath the surface, something was shifting.

The 1950s would bring new music, new freedoms, and new faces — and among them, a young man from Bengal whose café would help usher Penzance into the modern age.

This chapter sets the stage for that transformation.

Post-War Cornwall: A Landscape Of Recovery

In the late 1940s, Cornwall was still marked by the war:

- bomb damage in scattered places
- returning servicemen adjusting to civilian life
- families grieving losses
- industries rebuilding
- tourism only just beginning to reawaken

Penzance remained a working town with a strong sense of itself — shaped by fishing, hospitality, and the steady pulse of local trade.

Life was modest.
People knew their neighbours.
Children played in the streets.
Sundays were quiet.

And diversity was almost nonexistent.

A Town With Little Ethnic Diversity

Before the arrival of Makhan Lal Dass, many people in Penzance had never met anyone from outside Cornwall, let alone someone from India.

The town's population was overwhelmingly white and local.
Most families had lived in the area for generations.
The idea of migration — of people arriving from faraway places — felt distant, something that happened in cities, not in a Cornish harbour town.

This is what makes the Dass story so significant.

Their arrival wasn't just a family settling in a new place.
It was the beginning of a quiet cultural shift — one that would unfold not through politics or protest, but through cups of coffee, shared jokes, and the warm glow of a jukebox.

Youth Culture Before Cafés

Before Dass's Café, young people in Penzance had limited places to gather.

Their social world revolved around:

- the promenade
- the cinema
- church youth groups
- dances at the Winter Gardens
- occasional events at schools or halls

There were no dedicated youth cafés.
No jukeboxes.
No spaces where teenagers could claim a corner of the town as their own.

Young people were expected to behave, to be home early, to stay within the boundaries set by parents and teachers.

But the world was changing.

The Arrival Of New Ideas, New Music, New Possibilities

By the early 1950s, the first waves of American culture were reaching Cornwall:

- Rock 'n' roll records
- Hollywood films
- new fashions
- new attitudes toward youth

Teenagers were beginning to see themselves as a distinct generation — not just smaller versions of adults.

The arrival of a café with a jukebox — the first many had ever seen — would electrify this shift.

Dass's Café didn't just serve drinks.
It offered a new way of being young.

Why The Dass Story Matters

The story of Dass's Café is not simply the story of a business.

It is the story of:

- migration
- belonging
- community
- youth culture
- music
- memory
- and the quiet ways ordinary people shape the places they live

It is a story about how one family — arriving from thousands of miles away — became part of the fabric of a Cornish town.

It is a story about how a café became a landmark in the hearts of a generation.

And it begins here, in a Penzance on the cusp of change, waiting — without knowing it — for the sound of a jukebox to transform its streets.

Makhan Lal Dass: A Life Between Worlds

From Bengal to Britain: the journey that shaped a town

Introduction: A Quiet Pioneer

Long before his name became part of Penzance's everyday vocabulary — long before the jukebox, the café windows, the silver-service restaurant — Makhan Lal Dass was a young man standing at the edge of two worlds.

His life began in India during a time of political upheaval and global uncertainty. It would take him across continents, into the Royal Air Force, and eventually into the heart of a Cornish town that would become his home.

This chapter traces that journey — not as a grand epic, but as the story of a man whose steady determination shaped the lives of thousands without ever seeking recognition.

Early Life In India

Makhan Lal Dass was born in the early decades of the twentieth century, part of a generation raised in a country still under British rule.
His childhood would have been shaped by:

- a multilingual, multicultural environment
- the rise of Indian nationalism
- the growing movement for education and professional training abroad

He belonged to a cohort of young Indians who saw education as a pathway to opportunity — and who looked to Britain as the place where that future could be built.

This ambition would set the course for the rest of his life.

Migration To Britain: A Journey Of Possibility

In the 1930s or early 1940s, Makhan Dass made the journey to Britain — a long, expensive, and often daunting voyage for a young man from India.

He arrived not as a labourer, but as a student and trainee, part of a wave of South Asian men who came to Britain seeking:

- higher education
- technical training
- professional advancement
- a chance to build a new life

For many in Cornwall, this was an unfamiliar story.
Migration to the region was rare; migration from India was almost unheard of.

Makhan Dass was stepping into a world where he would be both visible and alone — and yet he carried himself with the quiet confidence of someone who knew why he had come.

The Raf Years (1942): Duty, Discipline & Character

In 1942, during the height of the Second World War, Makhan Dass appeared in *Indian Information*, a wartime magazine published by the Indian Embassy in the United States.

The article described him as:

- a Wireless Operator
- stationed at a flying-boat base in Scotland
- a young man who spent every spare moment reading aviation manuals
- ambitious, studious, and determined

This small archival fragment — rediscovered decades later — offers a rare glimpse into his early character.

It shows a man who:

- embraced responsibility
- valued learning
- adapted quickly to new environments
- served Britain at a time of global crisis

The RAF was a crucible of discipline and multicultural contact.
It exposed him to British life, British humour, British routines — and to the idea that he could build a future here.

Settling In Penzance: A New Life In A New Land

After the war, Makhan Dass made a decision that would shape the next four decades of his life:
he settled in Penzance.

For a young Indian man in the 1940s, this was an extraordinary choice.
Cornwall was remote, rural, and overwhelmingly white.
But it was also a place of opportunity — a town where a hardworking man could build something of his own.

He married a local Cornish woman, and together they began to raise a family.

For many people in Penzance, the Dass family were the first Asian family they had ever met.
Their presence was new, unfamiliar — and ultimately transformative.

The First Café: Mount Street Beginnings

Before the famous café on Market Jew Street, the Dass family opened a small café in a house at the bottom of Mount Street.

It was a modest operation:

- part home, part business
- a few tables
- simple food
- a warm welcome

But it quickly became a social point for local families.

Community members remember:

- mothers working there
- parents meeting there
- the café as a friendly, homely place
- the Dass children growing up in its rooms

This first café was more than a business.
It was the family's first foothold in the town — a place where they began to weave themselves into the daily life of Penzance.

A Man Of Presence, Not Spectacle

Across hundreds of community recollections, a consistent portrait emerges of Makhan Dass:

- kind
- firm when needed
- quietly humorous
- fair
- respected
- steady
- hardworking

He was not a man who sought attention.
He shaped the town through presence — through the café counter, the daily greetings, the watchful eye over the jukebox, the steady rhythm of work.

His life was not defined by grand gestures, but by the quiet constancy that builds trust.

The Beginning Of A Legacy

By the time the family moved the café to Market Jew Street in the early 1950s, Makhan Dass had already laid the foundations of a life that would become part of Penzance's collective memory.

He had:

- crossed continents
- served in the RAF
- built a family
- opened a business
- become part of a community that had never seen a family like his

The next chapters of his life — and of this book — will show how that café became a cultural landmark, a youth hub, and a place where generations of Penzance residents found friendship, music, and identity.

But it all begins with this journey:
a young man from Bengal, stepping into a new world, and quietly changing the history of a town.

The First Café: Mount Street Beginnings

Where the Dass story took root — a home, a business, a beginning

Introduction: Before The Landmark, There Was A Living Room

Long before the chrome tables and jukebox glow of Market Jew Street, the Dass family's first café lived inside a house — a modest, lived-in space at the bottom of Mount Street.
It was not designed to be iconic.
It was not meant to be a cultural landmark.
It was simply a way to begin.

And yet, in the memories of Penzance residents, this first café is where everything started:
the friendships, the family connections, the early encounters with a new culture, and the quiet weaving of the Dass name into the fabric of the town.

This chapter returns to that beginning — the small, warm, unassuming space where a family built its first foothold in Cornwall.

A House That Became A Café

The Mount Street café was unlike anything that would come later.
It was not a commercial premises.
It was a home — and a business — at the same time.

People remember:

- a front room turned into a serving space
- a few tables, close together
- the smell of cooking drifting from the family kitchen
- children running through the hallway
- neighbours dropping in for tea or a bite to eat

It was intimate, domestic, and unmistakably personal.
This was not a café you visited anonymously.
It was a place where you were seen, greeted, and remembered.

The First Customers: Mothers, Workers, Neighbours

The earliest customers were not teenagers or jukebox-hungry crowds.
They were:

- local mothers
- workers from nearby shops
- neighbours
- friends of friends
- people who knew the family, or wanted to

Several community members recall their mothers working there — a detail that speaks to the café's early integration into local life.

Others remember their parents meeting there, or stopping in on their way to work.

This was the Dass family's first introduction to Penzance — not through spectacle, but through everyday hospitality.

A Family At The Centre Of The Room

Because the café was also the family home, the Dass children grew up in the middle of it.

People remember:

- children playing in the back rooms
- siblings helping with small tasks
- the sound of family life mixing with the clatter of cups
- the warmth of a household that was always busy

This blending of home and business created a unique atmosphere — one that made the café feel less like a shop and more like a neighbour's kitchen.

It also meant that the Dass family was visible, present, and familiar to the community from the very beginning.

The First Asian Family Many Had Ever Met

For many in Penzance, the Dass family were the first Asian family they had ever encountered.
This early café became a place of firsts:

- the first time someone heard an Indian surname
- the first time someone saw a South Asian man running a business
- the first time children asked their parents questions about difference

- the first time neighbours learned to pronounce "Dass"

And yet, the memories show no sense of distance or suspicion.
Instead, people recall warmth, curiosity, and a sense of novelty that quickly turned into familiarity.

The café was not just a business — it was a bridge.

A Foothold In The Town

The Mount Street café gave the family:

- income
- stability
- visibility
- community connections
- a sense of belonging

It was here that Makhan Dass learned the rhythms of local life.
It was here that the family built relationships that would last decades.
It was here that the Dass name first became part of the town's vocabulary.

And it was here that the idea of a larger café — one that would become a cultural landmark — began to take shape.

The Transition To Market Jew Street

By the early 1950s, the family had outgrown the Mount Street café.

The town was changing.
Youth culture was emerging.
Music was becoming central to social life.
And the Dass family saw an opportunity.

They moved the business to Market Jew Street — a decision that would transform not only their own lives, but the social landscape of Penzance.
The next chapter tells that story.

Dass's Café on Market Jew Street

The cultural landmark that shaped a generation

Introduction: A New Address, A New Era

When the Dass family moved their café from Mount Street to Market Jew Street in the early 1950s, they were not simply relocating a business.
They were stepping into the centre of town life — into the flow of shoppers, schoolchildren, railway passengers, and the growing tide of youth culture.

Market Jew Street was the artery of Penzance.
And Dass's Café, perched near the railway station, became its pulse.

This chapter brings the reader into that space — the windows, the chrome, the jukebox glow — and shows how a modest café became a landmark in the hearts of a community.

The Location: Where Everything Happened

Market Jew Street was the perfect place for a café that would become a social crossroads.

People remember:

- the constant movement of shoppers
- the sound of buses and bicycles
- the railway station just down the slope
- WH Smith directly opposite
- Hicks hairdresser's next door
- the flow of teenagers passing by after school

It was a place where you could see everyone — and be seen by everyone.

For young people, this mattered.
For the Dass family, it meant visibility, footfall, and a place at the centre of town life.

The Café Layout: Chrome, Light & Modernity

The café itself was small, bright, and unmistakably modern for its time.

Community memories describe:

- chrome-edged tables
- posters of Elvis and Cliff Richard
- a long counter at the front
- a silver-service restaurant at the back
- the jukebox glowing in the corner
- large windows facing the street

Those windows became iconic.

Teenagers sat in them, elbows on the sill, watching the world go by.
People walking past could see who was inside — who was with whom, who was laughing, who was trying to look older than they were.

The windows made the café a stage.
And the young people of Penzance were its actors.

A Social Crossroads: Where Everyone Met

Dass's Café quickly became the meeting point for:

- school friends
- first dates
- Saturday crowds
- young workers on lunch breaks
- teenagers killing time before the cinema
- groups heading to the Winter Gardens or Railway Hotel

It was the place you went:

- before the pictures
- after the pictures
- before a dance
- after a dance
- when you had nowhere else to go
- when you wanted to feel part of something

People didn't just meet at Dass's Café.
They *became* themselves there.

The Atmosphere: Buzzing, Warm, A Little Bit Risqué

The café had a reputation — and young people loved it.

It was:

- lively
- slightly rebellious
- full of laughter
- full of music
- full of possibility

Parents sometimes warned their daughters not to go there.
Which, of course, made them go even more.

It wasn't dangerous.
It was simply *alive* — a place where teenagers could feel grown-up, independent, and part of a world bigger than school and home.

Mr Dass: The Watchful Eye Behind The Counter

Behind the counter stood Makhan Lal Dass — calm, observant, and quietly amused by the energy swirling around him.

People remember him:

- greeting customers with a nod
- keeping an eye on the jukebox
- scolding the boys who tried to hack it
- laughing at the banter
- maintaining order without ever raising his voice

He was part of the café's identity — a steady presence in a room full of youthful chaos.

His mixture of firmness and humour became legendary.

The Café As A Cultural Landmark

By the mid-1950s, Dass's Café was no longer just a business.
It was:

- a youth hub

- a music venue
- a social institution
- a rite of passage
- a place where memories were made

People still speak of it with affection decades later — not because of the food or the décor, but because of what it represented:

freedom, friendship, music, identity.

This chapter marks the beginning of the café's golden era — the years when it became the beating heart of Penzance youth culture.

The next chapter dives into that world fully.

Part II — The Café Years (1950s–1960s)

Youth Culture: The Golden Era

Where a generation found itself — and each other

Introduction: The Years That Still Glow In Memory

Ask anyone who grew up in Penzance in the 1950s or 60s where they spent their youth, and the answer comes quickly, often with a smile:

Dass's Café.

For an entire generation, it wasn't just a place to buy a drink.
It was where friendships formed, romances began, identities took shape, and the world suddenly felt bigger, brighter, and full of possibility.

This chapter brings that era to life — the rituals, the laughter, the rebellion, and the sense of belonging that made Dass's Café the beating heart of youth culture in postwar Penzance.

After-School Crowds: The Daily Rush

Every weekday afternoon, the café filled with schoolchildren still in uniform, bags slung over chairs, coins clutched in pockets.

They came for:

- a drink
- a song on the jukebox
- a chance to see who else was there
- a moment of freedom before heading home

The after-school rush became a ritual — a daily gathering that shaped friendships and routines.

For many, it was the first place they felt independent, even if only for an hour.

Saturday Rituals: The Social Highlight Of The Week

Saturdays were different.
Saturdays were electric.

Teenagers poured into the café in groups, dressed in their best, ready for a day that felt like a small adventure.

The rituals were almost universal:

- meet friends in town
- browse the shops
- head to Dass's Café
- sit in the windows
- watch the world go by
- plan the evening ahead

For many, Saturday at Dass's Café was the highlight of the week — a moment when the town felt alive and full of promise.

First Boyfriends, First Dates, First Glimpses Of Adulthood

Dass's Café was where countless young people experienced their first steps into romance.

People remember:

- shy glances across the room
- sitting close in the window seats
- sharing a drink
- waiting for a favourite song to play
- the thrill of being seen together

It was a place where teenagers could feel grown-up — not quite adults, but no longer children.

The café gave them a space to practice who they wanted to become.

The Café As A Rite Of Passage

For many young people, going to Dass's Café was a milestone.

It meant:

- you were old enough

- you were trusted enough
- you were part of the social world
- you belonged

Some parents disapproved.
Some teachers frowned.
Some church groups warned against it.

Which only made it more irresistible.

To step through the café door was to step into a new phase of life — one defined by music, friendship, and the intoxicating sense of freedom.

Parental Restrictions: "Off Bounds"

A recurring theme in community memory is the phrase:

"I wasn't allowed to go there."

Dass's Café had a reputation — not dangerous, but lively, modern, and slightly risqué.

Parents worried about:

- boys
- smoking
- loud music
- the café's location at the "bottom of town"
- the new culture of teenage independence

Girls, especially, were often told to stay away.

And yet, they went.

They went because everyone else was there.
They went because it was exciting.
They went because it was the place where life was happening.
The café became a quiet act of rebellion — a safe, joyful, everyday defiance.

Rebellion & Freedom: The Pull Of The Café

Dass's Café offered a kind of freedom that was rare in postwar Cornwall.

It was a place where:

- you could smoke without being caught (unless a teacher walked in)
- you could flirt
- you could laugh loudly
- you could play the same song over and over
- you could be yourself

The café wasn't just a building.
It was a boundary — the line between childhood and adulthood, between rules and independence.

Crossing that threshold felt like stepping into a new world.

The Windows: A Stage For Youth

The café's large front windows became iconic.

Teenagers sat in them like performers on a stage, watching the street and being watched in return.

People remember:

- leaning out to talk to friends passing by
- waving at boys on bicycles
- pretending not to notice someone they hoped would notice them
- feeling glamorous, grown-up, and part of something

The windows turned the café into a social theatre — and every teenager into a character in the unfolding drama of youth.

A Place Where Identities Were Formed

Looking back, many people describe Dass's Café as the place where they:

- found their friends
- discovered their taste in music
- learned confidence
- experienced first love
- felt part of a community
- shaped who they would become

It was not just a café.
It was a formative space — a crucible of identity.

The memories are warm, vivid, and enduring because the café was more than a location.
It was a feeling.

The Golden Era Begins

By the late 1950s, Dass's Café had become the centre of youth life in Penzance.

The next chapter explores the machine that made this possible — the glowing, humming, chrome-trimmed heart of the café:

the jukebox.

The Jukebox: Sound, Light & Identity

The glowing heart of Dass's Café — and of a generation

Introduction: The Machine That Changed Everything

If Dass's Café was the body of youth culture in 1950s and 60s Penzance, the jukebox was its beating heart.

People remember the café fondly.
They remember the windows, the chrome tables, the laughter.

But the jukebox —
that is remembered with *emotion.*

It was more than a machine.
It was a portal, a soundtrack, a symbol of modernity, and the centre of gravity for every young person who stepped through the café door.

This chapter tells its story.

The First Jukebox In Penzance

Many community members recall that Dass's Café had the first jukebox in the town.

In a postwar Cornwall still shaped by rationing and modest wages, the arrival of a jukebox felt like a glimpse of another world:

- American music
- electric sound
- chrome and colour
- youth independence
- the thrill of choosing your own soundtrack

It was modern.
It was glamorous.
It was irresistible.

And it changed the atmosphere of the café overnight.

The Machine Itself: Light, Chrome & Warmth

Memories of the jukebox are vivid and sensory.

People describe:

- the warm glow of its lights
- the chrome trim catching reflections
- the hum of valves warming up
- the click of the mechanism selecting a record
- the whirr as the arm lifted and dropped
- the rich, warm sound filling the café

Some remember the smell — that faint, warm scent of heated valves and dust, unmistakable to anyone who grew up with analogue machines.

It wasn't just heard.
It was *felt*.

The Balami E80 (1953): A Local Legend

One community member identified the model as a BALAMI E80, produced in Essex in the early 1950s.

Whether or not this was the exact model, the description matches the memories:

- curved glass front
- illuminated panels
- chrome grille
- 80-record capacity
- valve-driven sound

It was a machine built to be seen — and to be loved.

The Songs That Defined An Era

The jukebox brought the world into Penzance.

People remember specific songs with astonishing clarity:

1950s favourites

- Lonnie Donegan
- Fats Domino
- Everly Brothers

- Cliff Richard
- Elvis Presley
- "Hang Down Your Head Tom Dooley"
- "Cumberland Gap"
- "Apache"

1960s favourites

- The Beatles
- The Rolling Stones
- Dave Clark Five
- Brian Hyland

These songs weren't just background noise.
They were the soundtrack of first loves, friendships, rebellions, and Saturday afternoons.

Rituals Around The Machine

The jukebox created its own social choreography.

People remember:

- crowding around it in groups
- arguing over which song to play
- saving coins for a favourite track
- listening to the same record on repeat
- watching the mechanism move behind the glass
- waiting for "your" song to come on

It was a ritual — a shared experience that bound people together.

Jukebox Hacking: The Secret Art Of Free Plays

A legendary part of café folklore is the way some boys learned to make the jukebox play without coins.

They would:

- press the selector in a certain way
- tap the side panel
- or use a trick known only to the boldest

And every time they did, Mr Dass would appear behind them, half-annoyed, half-amused, delivering his famous line:

"You bloody buggers!"

This phrase appears again and again in community memories — a testament to how deeply it became part of the café's soundscape.

Music As Belonging

For many young people, the jukebox was the first place they felt a sense of identity.

Music became:

- a badge of belonging
- a way to express taste
- a way to impress friends
- a way to flirt
- a way to rebel
- a way to feel part of something bigger

The jukebox didn't just play songs.
It created community.

The Jukebox As A Symbol Of Modernity

In a town still shaped by tradition, the jukebox represented:

- the future
- the outside world
- the arrival of youth culture
- the beginning of a new social era

It was a machine, yes — but it was also a symbol.

A symbol of change.
A symbol of possibility.
A symbol of a generation stepping into its own.

The Heart Of The Café

Everything in Dass's Café revolved around the jukebox:

- the laughter
- the flirting
- the arguments
- the friendships
- the memories

It was the centre of the room, the centre of the era, and the centre of the story.

The next chapter explores another dimension of the café's world — the people who worked there, and how the café shaped their lives.

Working at the Café & Riviera Hotel

First jobs, silver service, and the hidden labour behind a cultural landmark

Introduction: Behind The Counter, Behind The Scenes

While Dass's Café is remembered for its jukebox, its windows, and its crowds of teenagers, there is another story woven through its history — the story of the people who worked there.

For many young women in Penzance, the café and the later Riviera Hotel were their first workplaces, their first taste of independence, and their first step into adult responsibility.

This chapter honours their labour, their memories, and the role they played in making the café what it was.

The Café As A Workplace

Behind the laughter and music, the café was a busy, demanding environment.

Workers remember:

- carrying heavy trays
- wiping down chrome tables
- clearing ashtrays
- taking orders from crowds of teenagers
- navigating the narrow space behind the counter
- learning to move quickly and gracefully

It was fast-paced, noisy, and sometimes chaotic — but it was also exciting.

For many, it was the first time they felt part of the adult world.

Waitresses: The Heart Of The Operation

The waitresses were central to the café's atmosphere.

Community memories describe them as:

- friendly
- efficient

- stylish
- confident
- part of the café's identity

Some were still in school.
Some were saving for holidays.
Some were working to support their families.

They remember:

- the thrill of earning their own money
- the camaraderie among staff
- the pride of being trusted with responsibility
- the fun of working in the liveliest place in town

For many young women, this was their first job — and it shaped their sense of independence.

The Kitchen: The Unsung Engine Room

Behind the scenes, the kitchen was a world of its own.

Workers recall:

- the heat
- the constant washing up
- the clatter of plates
- the smell of frying and baking
- the rhythm of preparing meals for a full café

It was hard work, but it was also a place of jokes, gossip, and shared stories.

The kitchen staff — often young women, sometimes older women, sometimes members of the Dass family — kept the café running smoothly.

Their labour made the social magic possible.

Wages, Free Meals & The Value Of Work

One of the most consistent memories is that Mr Dass paid well — and paid on time. Workers remember:

- fair wages
- free midday meals
- occasional treats
- the feeling of being respected

For many young women, this was their first experience of financial independence.

They used their wages to:

- buy clothes
- save for dances
- help at home
- enjoy small luxuries

The café didn't just give them a job.
It gave them agency.

The Riviera Hotel: A New Level Of Professionalism

By the 1960s, the Dass family expanded into the Riviera Hotel — a larger, more formal establishment with a silver-service restaurant.

This was a step up in every sense.

Workers remember:

- crisp uniforms
- polished cutlery
- formal table settings
- learning the etiquette of silver service
- serving tourists and locals alike
- the pride of mastering new skills

For many young women, working at the Riviera was a formative experience — a place where they learned professionalism, confidence, and poise.

Summer Jobs & Seasonal Work

The Riviera became a major employer during the summer months.

Teenagers and young adults remember:

- long shifts
- busy evenings
- laughter in the staff room
- friendships that lasted decades
- the thrill of earning more during tourist season

Some returned year after year.
Others moved on to new jobs, carrying the skills they learned with them.

The Riviera was a training ground — a place where young people learned how to work, how to manage responsibility, and how to carry themselves in the world.

Intergenerational Employment: A Family Tradition

One striking pattern in the archive is how many families had multiple members work for the Dass family.

People recall:

- sisters working together
- mothers and daughters both employed
- cousins joining during the summer
- friends recommending each other

The café and the Riviera became part of the town's employment landscape — a place where work was steady, fair, and respected.

Mr Dass As An Employer

Workers remember Makhan Dass with warmth and respect.

They describe him as:

- fair
- punctual with wages
- firm but kind
- appreciative of good work

- quietly humorous

He wasn't a distant boss.
He was present — behind the counter, in the kitchen, in the restaurant — guiding, watching, and supporting.

His leadership shaped the workplace culture, and his fairness is remembered decades later.

The Café As A Social World

For the young people who worked there, the café was more than a job.

It was:

- a social hub
- a place to make friends
- a place to meet people
- a place to grow up
- a place to feel part of something

Many workers describe their time at the café or the Riviera as some of the happiest years of their youth.

The work was hard.
The hours were long.
But the memories are warm, vivid, and cherished.

The Hidden Labour Behind A Landmark

Dass's Café is remembered for its music, its atmosphere, and its role in youth culture.
But behind that magic was the labour of dozens of young women and men who kept the place running.
Their work — often invisible, often unacknowledged — was essential to the café's success.
This chapter honours them.
The next chapter turns to the Dass children themselves — the generation who grew up between cultures, between worlds, and at the centre of a town's social life.

PART III — FAMILY, MUSIC & COMMUNITY

The Dass Children: Growing Up Between Cultures

Five children, two worlds, one town that remembers them still

Introduction: A Family At The Heart Of A Community

Behind the counter, behind the jukebox, behind the laughter and the crowds, there was a family — a large, lively, mixed-heritage family whose presence shaped the social life of Penzance for decades.

Bina
Ronjon
Mac.
Robbie.
Anna.

Their childhoods unfolded in the middle of a café that never slept, a home that doubled as a workplace, and a town that was learning, slowly and quietly, what multicultural Britain could look like.

This chapter tells their story — not as a single narrative, but as a tapestry woven from community memory, affection, and the everyday moments that made the Dass children part of Penzance's identity.

Growing Up In A Café: A Childhood In Motion

For the Dass children, home was never separate from the world outside.

They grew up:

- in the rooms above the café
- in the kitchen where meals were prepared
- in the doorway where customers came and went
- in the windows where teenagers gathered
- in the hum of conversation and clatter of cups

Their childhood was public, social, and full of movement.

People remember seeing them:

- running up and down the stairs
- helping behind the counter
- chatting with regulars
- laughing with friends
- slipping between family life and café life with ease

They were part of the café's atmosphere — familiar faces in a familiar place.

Between Two Cultures: A Mixed-Heritage Childhood

The Dass children grew up between worlds:

- Indian heritage from their father
- Cornish heritage from their mother
- British schooling
- a multicultural household
- a town that had never seen a family like theirs

For many in Penzance, the Dass children were the first mixed-heritage children they had ever known.

And yet, the memories show no sense of distance or exclusion.
Instead, people recall them with warmth, affection, and a sense of familiarity.

They were simply part of the town — part of the landscape of daily life.

School Life: Friendships, Classrooms & Local Roots

The children attended local schools:

- St Paul's
- Lescudjack
- and other primary schools in the area

Classmates remember:

- sitting next to them in lessons
- walking home together
- playing in the playground
- sharing jokes and stories
- seeing them later behind the café counter

School was where the Dass children became woven into the social fabric of their generation.

They were not outsiders.
They were friends, classmates, teammates — part of the everyday life of Penzance's youth.

Bina: A Bridge Between Family & Community

Bina is remembered with particular affection.

People recall:

- her warmth
- her friendliness
- her later work at the hospital
- her deep roots in the community

She represents the way the Dass family became part of the town's everyday life — not just through the café, but through service, care, and connection.

Ronjon: Music, Charisma & A Brief Brilliance

Ronjon's story is told fully in the next chapter, but here he appears as the charismatic, musically gifted younger son whose presence left a lasting impression.

People remember:

- his love of blues records
- his early bands
- his talent
- his warmth
- the sadness of his early death

He is one of the most vividly remembered figures in the archive.

Mac (Makan): The Steady Hand & Future Publican

Mac, the eldest son, grew into a calm, reliable presence — someone who would later take the family business into a new era with Mac's Bar in the 1980s.

People remember him as:

- friendly
- grounded
- part of the café's daily rhythm

His later role in the town's nightlife would continue the Dass legacy into a new Generation.

Robbie (Robinda): Quiet, Kind, Well-Liked

Robbie is remembered as gentle and well-liked.

Classmates recall:
- his kindness
- his easy smile
- his presence in the café and around town

He was part of the family's steady, familiar presence in Penzance.

Anna: Bright, Social, Part Of The Café's Life

Anna appears in memories as lively, social, and part of the café's atmosphere.

People remember:
- her presence behind the counter
- her friendships
- her role in the family's public life

She was part of the generation that grew up in the café's golden era.

Friends, Neighbours & The Extended Social World

The Dass children were not isolated.

They grew up surrounded by:
- neighbours
- school friends
- café regulars
- local musicians
- staff from the café and Riviera

- families who lived nearby

People remember:

- playing with them in the street
- visiting the café to see them
- attending parties or gatherings
- seeing them at dances, youth clubs, and school events

The Dass children were part of the town's social world — visible, familiar, and woven into the memories of hundreds of people.

A Family That Belonged

What emerges from the archive is a portrait of a family that was not simply *in* Penzance, but *of* Penzance.

The children grew up:

- between cultures
- between identities
- between home and café
- between tradition and modernity

And yet, they belonged — fully, naturally, and without question.

Their presence helped shape the town's understanding of community, diversity, and belonging long before such conversations had names.

Ronjon Dass: Music, Talent & Memory

The brief brilliance of a young man whose voice still echoes in Penzance

Introduction: A Name Spoken With Warmth

Among all the names that surface in the community memory archive, one appears with a particular tenderness:
Ronjon Dass.

He is remembered not only as the son of Makhan Lal Dass, but as a young man whose musical talent, charisma, and warmth left a lasting impression on those who knew him.

His life was short.
His impact was deep.
And his memory remains vivid, decades later.

This chapter gathers those fragments — musical, emotional, and historical — to honour a young man who shone brightly in the cultural life of postwar Penzance.

A Child Of Two Worlds

Ronjon grew up in a household that blended Indian heritage with Cornish life.

His father's café was a hub of youth culture, music, and social energy.
His mother's Cornish roots connected him to the local community.
His siblings surrounded him with warmth, humour, and the everyday chaos of a large family.

People remember him as:

- "a great chap"
- "a great character"
- "full of life"
- "someone everyone liked"

He belonged fully to Penzance — and yet he carried a musical sensibility that reached far beyond it.

A Musical Ear: Blues, Records & Influence

One of the most striking details in the archive is Ronjon's love of blues records, especially artists like Lead Belly.

This was unusual for the time.

While many teenagers were listening to chart hits, Ronjon was absorbing the raw, soulful sound of American blues — music that would later shape the early British rock scene.

He wasn't just listening.
He was learning.

His musical taste placed him at the forefront of a cultural shift that was only just beginning to reach Cornwall.

Ronjon & The Trident: The First Band

Ronjon's first known band was Ronjon and the Trident, formed with schoolmates from Lescudjack.

Bandmates included:

- Dick Gwenip
- Alan Manning (drums)

People remember:

- "They played quite a few venues in Penzance."
- "They were good — they had something."
- "Ronjon loved performing."

This was the era when local bands were springing up across Cornwall, inspired by the explosion of youth culture.

Ronjon was part of that wave — a young man with a voice, a guitar, and a presence that drew people in.

The Vandells: A New Sound, A New Era

Community members also recall that Ronjon and the Trident evolved into The Vandells, one of the local bands of the time.

Key musicians included:

- Bob Turner (lead guitar)
- Dennis Wood (also played with The Buccaneers)

The Vandells played in:

- dance halls
- pubs
- youth clubs
- community events

For many, these bands were the soundtrack of their teenage years.

Ronjon's voice and charisma were central to that sound.

A Young Man Remembered With Affection

Across the archive, Ronjon is remembered with warmth and sadness.

People say:

- "He was a great chap."
- "A sad loss."
- "A great character."
- "Everyone liked him."

These are not distant recollections.
They are the words of people who knew him, laughed with him, listened to him sing, and watched him grow up.

He was talented.
He was kind.
He was full of potential.

A Life Cut Short

Ronjon died very young, just after turning nineteen.

The community remembers this as a moment of deep sadness — a shock that rippled through friends, family, and the local music scene.

People recall:

- "We were all devastated."
- "It was a very sad time."
- "He was deeply cut up about a breakup."
- "A great loss."

His death left a silence where music had been.

This chapter honours his memory without dwelling on the circumstances — focusing instead on the life he lived, the music he made, and the people he touched.

The Afterlife Of Memory

Even decades later, people still speak of Ronjon with:

- affection
- respect
- sadness
- admiration

His name appears in conversations about:

- the early music scene
- the café
- the jukebox
- the Dass family
- the youth culture of the 1950s and 60s

He is remembered not as a tragic figure, but as a bright, talented young man whose presence shaped the lives of those around him.

Ronjon's Place In The Story Of Penzance

Ronjon Dass represents something larger than himself:

- the rise of youth culture
- the birth of local bands
- the blending of cultures
- the energy of postwar modernity
- the fragility of young lives
- the power of community memory

His story is inseparable from the story of Dass's Café — a place where music, youth, and identity converged.

Conclusion: A Brief Brilliance

Ronjon's life was short, but it was full of music, friendship, and promise.

He was part of a pioneering family, part of a changing town, and part of a generation discovering its voice.

His voice may no longer be heard, but the echoes remain — in the memories of those who loved him, in the stories passed down, and in the cultural history of Penzance.

The next chapter widens the lens again, exploring the wider family and the social networks that made the Dass name part of the town's fabric.

The Wider Family & Social Networks

How the Dass family became woven into the everyday life of a town

Introduction: A Family That Belonged To The Community

The Dass story is not only the story of a café or a jukebox or a generation of teenagers.
It is also the story of a family — a large, mixed-heritage, hardworking family whose presence touched many corners of Penzance.

This chapter explores the wider network of relationships that surrounded the Dass family:
the siblings, the in-laws, the grandchildren, the neighbours, the friends, and the countless people who felt connected to them in ways big and small.

It is a chapter about belonging — not as an abstract idea, but as a lived, everyday reality.

The Family At The Centre Of It All

The Dass family was not a distant or private household.
They were visible, approachable, and deeply rooted in the town's daily life.

People remember:

- seeing them in the café
- chatting with them in the street
- attending school with them
- working alongside them
- meeting them in pubs, shops, and workplaces
- watching them grow up, marry, and raise children

The family was part of the town's rhythm — familiar, trusted, and woven into its social landscape.

Bina: Care, Community & A Life Of Service

Among the siblings, Bina stands out in community memory for her later work at the hospital.

People recall:

- her kindness
- her professionalism
- her warmth
- her ability to put people at ease

Her role in healthcare deepened the family's connection to the town.
She became part of the intimate, everyday moments of people's lives — births, illnesses, recoveries, and the quiet conversations that happen in hospital corridors.

Bina represents the way the Dass family moved beyond the café and into the broader fabric of community care.

Jimmy Gibson: A Well-Known Local Figure

Another name that appears in the archive is Jimmy Gibson, connected to the family through marriage.

People remember him as:

- sociable
- well-liked
- part of the local pub and social scene
- someone who fit naturally into the Dass family's world

His presence shows how the family's social network expanded outward, linking them to other well-known local families and circles.

The Grandchildren: Ben, Simon & A New Generation

The next generation — including Ben and Simon — carried the family's presence into the 1970s, 80s, and beyond.

People remember:

- seeing them around town
- their friendships
- their connection to the café and later Mac's Bar
- the continuation of the Dass name in local life

The grandchildren represent continuity — the way the family's story extended into new eras of Penzance's social history.

Extended Family & Social Connections

The Dass family's network was wide and varied.

People recall:

- cousins visiting
- family gatherings
- neighbours who became lifelong friends
- staff who felt like extended family
- musicians, waitresses, and regulars who stayed connected for decades

The café was the centre of this network, but the relationships extended far beyond its walls.

The Family As Part Of The Town's Fabric

What emerges from the archive is a portrait of a family that was not simply *present* in Penzance, but *embedded* in it.

They were part of:

- the workforce
- the music scene
- the social life
- the healthcare system
- the nightlife
- the everyday routines of ordinary people

Their story is not one of outsiders trying to fit in.
It is the story of a family who became part of the town's identity.

A Community That Remembered Them

Decades later, people still speak of the Dass family with:

- affection
- respect
- gratitude
- humour
- nostalgia

These memories are not just about the café.
They are about the people who ran it — the family whose presence shaped the lives of those around them.

Conclusion: A Family Woven Into Memory

The Dass family's story is not only about migration or business or music.
It is about relationships — the countless threads of connection that tie a family to a place.

This chapter honours those threads.

The next chapter moves the story into a new era — the 1960s and 70s — when the Riviera Hotel became the family's next major venture, and the café evolved once again.

Part IV - Transition & Legacy (1970s–1980s)

The Riviera Years

Silver service, summer seasons, and the evolution of a family business

Introduction: A New Chapter In A Changing Town

By the 1960s, Penzance was changing.

Tourism was growing.
Youth culture was evolving.
The town was becoming more outward-looking, more connected to the wider world.

And the Dass family — already well-established through their café on Market Jew Street — stepped into this new era with a bold expansion:
the Riviera Hotel.

This chapter explores the Riviera years: a period of professionalism, hospitality, and community connection that carried the Dass legacy into a new generation.

The Riviera Hotel: A Step Into Formal Hospitality

The Riviera was more than a café.
It was a full hotel and restaurant — a larger, more ambitious venture that required:

- trained staff
- formal service
- a broader clientele
- new skills
- new routines

For the Dass family, it was a natural evolution.
For the town, it became a familiar landmark — a place where locals and visitors alike gathered for meals, celebrations, and summer evenings.

Silver Service: Professionalism & Pride

One of the most vivid memories from this era is the silver-service restaurant at the back of the Riviera.

Workers recall:

- crisp white uniforms
- polished cutlery
- folded napkins
- formal table settings
- learning the etiquette of serving from the left and clearing from the right
- the pride of mastering a professional skill

For many young women, this was their first experience of formal hospitality work.

It taught them:

- confidence
- poise
- responsibility
- teamwork
- how to carry themselves in adult spaces

The Riviera was not just a workplace.
It was a training ground.

A Busy, Buzzing Summer Season

Tourism brought a new rhythm to the Riviera.

Workers remember:

- long summer evenings
- full dining rooms
- tourists from across Britain
- laughter spilling out into the street
- the excitement of earning more during the season
- friendships formed in the rush of service

The Riviera became a seasonal hub — a place where local teenagers worked alongside older staff, learning from each other and sharing stories.

For many, these summers remain some of the happiest memories of their youth.

A Place For Celebration & Community Events

The Riviera wasn't only a workplace.
It was also a venue for:

- wedding receptions
- family gatherings
- birthday parties
- community dinners
- special occasions

People remember:

- dancing
- speeches
- laughter
- the warm glow of the dining room
- the sense of occasion that filled the space

These events deepened the family's connection to the town.
The Riviera became part of the social fabric — a place where life's milestones were celebrated.

The Dass Family As Hosts

Throughout the Riviera years, the Dass family remained at the centre of the operation.

People remember:

- Makhan Dass overseeing the business with calm authority
- family members helping in the kitchen or restaurant
- the children moving between café, home, and hotel
- the sense that the Riviera was both a business and a family endeavour

Their presence gave the hotel a warmth that guests remembered.

It wasn't corporate.
It wasn't impersonal.
It was a family business — and people felt that.

Changing Clientele, Changing Times

The 1960s and 70s brought shifts in:

- fashion
- music
- social norms
- tourism patterns
- the expectations of young people

The Riviera adapted.

It welcomed:

- tourists in summer
- locals in winter
- young couples
- families
- groups heading out for the evening

The café on Market Jew Street remained the youth hub, but the Riviera became the family's more formal, grown-up space — a sign of their success and their evolving role in the town.

The Riviera As A Bridge Between Eras

The Riviera years sit at a crossroads in the Dass story.

They mark:

- the end of the café's golden era
- the beginning of a more professional hospitality venture
- the transition from 1950s youth culture to 1970s nightlife
- the foundation for what would become Mac's Bar in the 1980s

The Riviera was the bridge — the place where the family's story expanded, matured, and prepared for its next chapter.

Conclusion: A Legacy Of Hospitality

The Riviera Hotel represents a period of growth, professionalism, and community connection.

It was a place where:

- young people learned to work
- families celebrated milestones
- tourists discovered Penzance
- the Dass family deepened their roots in the town

The next chapter moves into the 1980s — a new era of music, nightlife, and cultural change — with Mac's Bar, the final evolution of the Dass family's presence in Penzance's social life.

Mac's Bar: A New Generation

Punk, Stella, 80s music, and the final evolution of a family legacy

Introduction: A New Era, A New Sound

By the late 1970s and early 1980s, Penzance was changing again.

The jukebox era of the 1950s and 60s had given way to:

- punk
- new wave
- louder nights
- later hours
- a new kind of youth culture

And into this shifting landscape stepped Mac Dass, the eldest son, carrying the family legacy into a new generation with a venue that would become iconic in its own right:

Mac's Bar.

This chapter explores the atmosphere, the music, the characters, and the memories of a place that defined nightlife for a whole new wave of young people.

Mac Dass: The Steady Hand Of A New Era

Mac had grown up in the café.
He had watched the crowds, learned the rhythms of hospitality, and absorbed the family's instinct for creating social spaces.

People remember him as:

- calm
- friendly
- reliable
- part of the town's everyday life

When he opened Mac's Bar, he wasn't just starting a business.
He was continuing a family tradition — adapting it to a new cultural moment.

The Atmosphere: Louder, Darker, More Electric

Mac's Bar was very different from the bright, chrome-trimmed café of the 1950s.

People remember:

- dimmer lights
- louder music
- a more adult crowd
- the smell of beer and cigarettes
- laughter spilling out onto the street
- the energy of the 1980s nightlife scene

It was a place where:

- punks gathered
- couples met
- friends started their nights
- locals mixed with visitors
- the jukebox played a new generation's soundtrack

Mac's Bar wasn't nostalgic.
It was contemporary — a reflection of its time.

The 80s Jukebox: A New Soundtrack

Just as the original café had its jukebox, Mac's Bar had its own — filled with the music of the era.

People remember:

- punk tracks
- new wave hits
- 80s anthems
- songs that defined nights out

The jukebox was still central — but the sound had changed.

Where the 1950s jukebox glowed with warmth and chrome, the 1980s jukebox pulsed with sharper edges, brighter colours, and a new kind of energy.

Stella, Laughter & Nightlife Culture

One detail appears again and again in community memory:

Stella.

Mac's Bar became known for:

- pints of Stella
- lively crowds
- late nights
- the kind of laughter that comes from shared stories and loud music

People remember:

- first dates
- birthday celebrations
- nights that blurred into early mornings
- friendships forged over drinks and jukebox songs

Mac's Bar was not glamorous.
It was real — a place where people relaxed, let loose, and felt part of something.

A Continuity Of Presence

Even though the atmosphere was different, Mac's Bar carried forward the spirit of the original café:

- a place to meet
- a place to belong
- a place where music mattered
- a place where the Dass name meant welcome

The family's presence in Penzance's social life did not fade with time.
It adapted — from café to hotel to bar — always meeting the needs of the moment.

The End Of An Era, The Beginning Of Memory

By the late 1980s, the Dass family's direct involvement in Penzance's hospitality scene began to wind down.

But the memories remained.

People still speak of Mac's Bar with:

- humour
- affection
- nostalgia
- a sense of continuity

It was the final chapter in a decades-long story of how one family shaped the social life of a town.

Conclusion: A Legacy That Evolved With The Times

Mac's Bar represents:

- the adaptability of the Dass family
- the evolution of youth culture
- the continuity of community spaces
- the way each generation finds its own soundtrack

From Mount Street to Market Jew Street, from the Riviera to Mac's Bar, the Dass story is one of transformation — always rooted in hospitality, music, and connection.

The next part of the book steps back from the narrative and explores the geography, memory, and heritage that frame the Dass legacy.

Part V — Memory, Place & Heritage

The Geography of Memory

Mapping the streets, landmarks, and social circuits that shaped the Dass story

Introduction: Memory Is A Map

Community memory is not abstract.
It lives in places — in streets, corners, shopfronts, and buildings that hold the echoes of laughter, music, and everyday life.

The Dass story is inseparable from the geography of Penzance.
To understand the café, the family, and their legacy, we must walk the streets where their story unfolded.

This chapter maps those places — not as they are now, but as they live in memory.

Mount Street: Where It All Began

Before the jukebox, before Market Jew Street, before the Riviera, there was Mount Street.

People remember:

- the house-café hybrid
- the smell of cooking drifting into the street
- neighbours stopping in for tea
- the Dass children running in and out
- the warmth of a family home that doubled as a business

Mount Street is the root of the story — the first foothold, the first welcome, the first connection between the Dass family and the town.

Market Jew Street: The Heart Of The Story

If Mount Street was the root, Market Jew Street was the bloom.

This was the café everyone remembers:

- the windows

- the chrome tables
- the jukebox glowing in the corner
- the crowds of teenagers
- the hum of conversation spilling onto the pavement

Market Jew Street was the artery of Penzance — and the café was its pulse.

People remember:
- WH Smith directly opposite
- Hicks hairdresser's next door
- the slope down to the railway station
- the constant movement of shoppers and schoolchildren

It was the perfect place for a youth hub — visible, central, alive.

The Railway Hotel / Longboat: The Nightlife Circuit

For many young people, the café was only the beginning of a night out.

The next stop was often:
- The Railway Hotel (later The Longboat)
- The Winter Gardens
- The Cornish Arms

These places formed a social circuit:
1. Meet at Dass's Café
2. Play a song on the jukebox
3. Walk down to the Railway Hotel
4. End the night at the Winter Gardens

The café was the gateway — the place where the night began.

Winter Gardens: Dances, Music & Youth Culture

The Winter Gardens was one of the main venues for dances, concerts, and social events.

People remember:
- walking there in groups
- dancing to live bands

- seeing local musicians perform
- the excitement of Saturday nights

The café and the Winter Gardens were linked — one fed into the other, creating a rhythm of youth culture that defined the era.

Wh Smith & Hicks Hairdresser's: Landmarks Of Memory

Two landmarks appear repeatedly in community recollections:

- WH Smith, directly opposite the café
- Hicks hairdresser's, next door

These places anchored the café in the mental map of the town.

People remember:

- leaning out of the café windows to watch people coming out of WH Smith
- meeting friends outside Hicks
- using these landmarks to describe where the café was

Memory is spatial — and these landmarks are part of the story.

The Social Circuit Of Youth

The geography of the Dass story is also the geography of youth culture.

People remember moving through the town in patterns:

- after school → café
- Saturday morning → shops → café
- Saturday night → café → Railway Hotel → Winter Gardens
- summer evenings → promenade → café

These circuits created a shared experience — a sense of belonging rooted in place.

Disappearing Landmarks, Enduring Memory

Many of the places in this chapter have changed:

- shopfronts replaced
- pubs renamed
- buildings demolished

- streets modernised

But in memory, they remain vivid.

The café may be gone, but the geography of memory is intact — carried in the stories of those who lived it.

Conclusion: A Map Of Belonging

The Dass story is not only about people.
It is about place — the streets, buildings, and landmarks that shaped a generation.

This chapter maps those places not as they are now, but as they were lived:

- full of music
- full of laughter
- full of youth
- full of life

The next chapter turns from geography to memory itself — exploring the 281 recollections that form the backbone of this book.

Community Memory Archive (1950s–2023)

What 281 recollections reveal about a café, a family, and a town

Introduction: A Living Archive Of Voices

Between 2014 and 2023, hundreds of people in Penzance shared their memories of Dass's Café, the Riviera Hotel, Mac's Bar, and the Dass family.
These recollections — 281 in total, from more than 175 individuals — form one of the richest community memory archives ever assembled for a single local business in Cornwall.

This chapter brings those voices together.

It does not attempt to flatten them into a single narrative.
Instead, it honours their diversity, their emotion, and their collective power to reconstruct a vanished world.

The Archive: What It Is And Why It Matters

The archive is:

- multi-generational
- multi-decadal
- emotionally rich
- socially revealing
- historically significant

It spans memories from the 1950s to the 1980s, and reflections posted online between 2014 and 2023.
It includes:

- youth culture
- music
- work
- migration
- family life
- grief
- humour
- belonging

Together, these memories form a mosaic — each piece small, but essential to the whole.

Thematic Clusters: What People Remember Most

Across the 281 recollections, certain themes appear again and again.

1. Youth Culture & Social Life (150+ memories)

The café was the beating heart of teenage life.
People remember:

- after-school crowds
- Saturday rituals
- first dates
- sitting in the windows
- feeling grown-up for the first time

This is the strongest theme in the entire archive.

2. The Jukebox & Music Culture (120+ memories)

The jukebox is remembered with extraordinary clarity.
People recall:

- specific songs
- the glow of the lights
- the warmth of the valves
- jukebox hacking
- Mr Dass's famous line

Music was the emotional centre of the café.

3. Employment & Working Life (60+ memories)

Many young women had their first job at the café or Riviera.
They remember:

- wages
- free meals
- silver service
- camaraderie
- learning confidence

Work shaped lives as much as music did.

4. Family Connections (80+ memories)

People remember:

- the Dass children
- the parents
- the grandchildren
- in-laws
- neighbours

The family was woven into the town's social fabric.

5. Geography & Place (90+ memories)

Memory is spatial.
People recall:

- Market Jew Street
- Mount Street
- WH Smith
- Hicks hairdresser's
- the Railway Hotel
- the Winter Gardens

These places anchor the story.

Emotional Patterns: How People Remember

The emotional tone of the archive is overwhelmingly positive.

Warm Nostalgia — Very High

People speak of "happy days," "halcyon days," and "the best years of my youth."

Affection — High

For Mr Dass, for the jukebox, for friends, for the era.

Humour — Medium

Jukebox tricks, being dragged out by parents, teachers catching kids smoking.

Belonging — High

The café was an identity anchor — a place where people felt part of something.

Rebellion — Medium

Sneaking in underage, ignoring parental bans, pushing boundaries.

Loss — Low–Medium

Ronjon's death, the passing of youth, the disappearance of landmarks.

These emotions give the archive its depth and humanity.

Gendered Memory: Who Remembers What

The archive reveals a striking pattern:

- Women provided richer emotional detail, sensory memory, and social context.
- Men contributed more to music history, band details, and structural information.

This duality enriches the archive — offering both emotional texture and historical specificity.

The Café As A Social Institution

The data confirms what the stories suggest:

- Dass's Café was the single most important youth hub in Penzance in the 1950s–60s.
- It was a site of early multicultural contact.
- It shaped the lives of young women through employment.
- It was a "forbidden zone" for girls — which made it irresistible.
- It was remembered with warmth, humour, and affection.

The café was not just a business.
It was a cultural institution.

The Power Of Memory: Why These Recollections Matter

Community memory is not always precise.
It is emotional, subjective, and shaped by time.

But it is also:

- truthful in feeling
- rich in detail
- socially revealing
- historically invaluable

These memories show how ordinary places become extraordinary through the lives lived within them.

They show how a café can become:

- a rite of passage
- a meeting place
- a cultural landmark
- a symbol of belonging

And they show how the Dass family — migrants, pioneers, hosts — became part of the town's identity.

Conclusion: A Chorus Of Voices

The Community Memory Archive is not a single story.
It is a chorus — hundreds of voices, each carrying a piece of the past.

Together, they reconstruct a world that no longer exists, but which lives on in memory.

Migration, Belonging & the First Asian Family in Penzance

What it meant — and still means — to be pioneers of multicultural life in a Cornish town

Introduction: A Quiet Revolution

When Makhan Lal Dass settled in Penzance in the 1940s, he did something quietly revolutionary.

He became part of a town that had almost no ethnic diversity.
He married a local woman.
He raised a mixed-heritage family.
He opened a café that would become the centre of youth culture.
He lived his life in full view of a community that had never seen a family like his.

This chapter explores the significance of that presence — not through theory or abstraction, but through the lived experiences preserved in the community memory archive.

The First Asian Family Many Had Ever Met

For many people in Penzance, the Dass family were the first Asian family they encountered in their lives.

This was not a city.
This was not a multicultural hub.
This was a rural Cornish town in the mid-twentieth century.

And yet, the memories show:

- no hostility
- no exclusion
- no sense of "otherness"

Instead, people recall:

- curiosity
- warmth
- familiarity
- affection

The Dass family became part of the town's everyday life — not through assimilation, but through presence.

Migration As Everyday Life, Not Drama

Migration stories are often told as dramatic journeys of struggle or conflict.

The Dass story is different.

It is a story of:

- quiet determination
- steady work
- building a family
- running a business
- becoming part of a community

There is no spectacle here.
There is dignity, routine, and the slow weaving of belonging.

This is what makes the story powerful.

The Café As A Site Of Early Multicultural Contact

Dass's Café was not just a business.
It was a cultural meeting point.

For many young people, it was:

- the first time they heard an Indian surname
- the first time they saw a South Asian man running a business
- the first time they interacted with someone from a different cultural background

These encounters were not formal or structured.
They were everyday moments:

- ordering a drink
- being told off for jukebox tricks
- chatting at the counter
- seeing the children grow up

This is how multiculturalism often begins — not with policy, but with cups of tea and shared laughter.

The Blending Of Cultures: A Family Between Worlds

The Dass children grew up between cultures:

- Indian heritage
- Cornish heritage
- British schooling
- a multicultural household
- a public life in the café

Their presence helped normalise diversity in a town that had never experienced it before.

People remember them not as "different," but as:

- classmates
- friends
- neighbours
- familiar faces in the café

Their mixed-heritage identity became part of the town's identity.

Community Acceptance: A Rare And Important Story

One of the most striking findings in the archive is the absence of negative memories.

People speak of the family with:

- respect
- affection
- gratitude
- humour

This is not to say that racism did not exist in Britain at the time — it did, and often violently.

But the Dass story shows something else:

the possibility of belonging in a place where difference was new.

It shows how communities can embrace change through everyday relationships.

It shows how migration can become part of local history, not as an exception, but as a thread in the fabric.

The Significance Of Their Presence

The Dass family's presence in Penzance matters because it represents:

- early multicultural life in rural Cornwall
- the blending of cultures long before such conversations were common
- the role of small businesses in shaping social change
- the power of everyday interactions to build belonging
- the importance of visibility in transforming community identity

Their story challenges assumptions about rural Britain.
It shows that diversity did not arrive suddenly in the 21st century.
It was already here — in cafés, in families, in friendships, in music.

The Legacy Of Belonging

Today, the Dass family is remembered not as outsiders, but as part of Penzance's heritage.

Their legacy lives in:

- the memories of those who grew up in the café
- the stories passed down through families
- the affection expressed in hundreds of recollections
- the cultural history of the town

Belonging is not something that happens overnight.
It is built through presence, work, kindness, and the simple act of being part of a place.

The Dass family embodied that.

Conclusion: A Story Of Quiet Transformation

The Dass story is not only about migration.
It is about:

- acceptance

- community
- identity
- the blending of cultures
- the power of everyday life to create change

It is a story of quiet transformation — one that shaped a town without fanfare, without conflict, and without seeking recognition.

The next chapter brings the book to its close, reflecting on what this story teaches us about history, memory, and the meaning of belonging.

PART VI — CONCLUSION

Legacy: What the Dass Story Teaches Us

How one family, one café, and one generation shaped the identity of a town

Introduction: A Story That Outlived Its Walls

Dass's Café no longer stands on Market Jew Street.
The jukebox is gone.
The chrome tables have vanished.
The windows where teenagers once sat are part of another building, another business, another time.

And yet — the café lives on.
It lives in the memories of hundreds of people.
It lives in the stories passed down through families.
It lives in the emotional landscape of Penzance.
It lives in the way people still speak of "Dass's" as if it were yesterday.

This chapter reflects on what that legacy means — not only for the town, but for anyone who has ever found belonging in an ordinary place made extraordinary by the people within it.

The Power Of Everyday Lives

History often focuses on grand events, famous figures, and dramatic moments.

But the Dass story shows something different:

that everyday lives can shape a community just as profoundly.

Makhan Lal Dass did not set out to change Penzance.
He opened a café.
He worked hard.
He raised a family.
He created a space where people felt welcome.

And in doing so, he changed the social landscape of a town.

The legacy of Dass's Café is a reminder that history is not only made in parliaments and palaces.
It is made in cafés, kitchens, workplaces, and the small rituals of daily life.

The Café As A Cultural Institution

Dass's Café was not just a business.
It was:

- a youth centre
- a music venue
- a meeting place
- a rite of passage
- a social crossroads
- a symbol of modernity

It shaped the identity of a generation.

People learned who they were in that café.
They found friends, fell in love, rebelled, laughed, and grew up.

The café's legacy teaches us that cultural institutions do not need grand architecture or official status.
They need people — and the freedom to be themselves.

The Importance Of Preserving Community Memory

The 281 recollections that form the backbone of this book are more than nostalgia.
They are a form of heritage.

They show:

- how memory works
- what people value
- how communities remember themselves
- how ordinary places become extraordinary

Without these memories, the story of Dass's Café would be lost.
With them, it becomes part of the town's cultural archive.
This book is not just a history.
It is an act of preservation.

The Dass Family's Place In Local History

The Dass family were pioneers — not through activism or public declarations, but through presence.

They were:

- the first Asian family many people ever met
- employers of dozens of young women
- hosts to generations of teenagers
- part of the town's music scene
- part of its nightlife
- part of its everyday life

Their story is a reminder that migration is not only an urban phenomenon.
It happens in small towns, in quiet streets, in cafés and kitchens.

And when it does, it reshapes the meaning of community.

Identity, Belonging & Change

The Dass story teaches us that belonging is not static.
It is created through:

- relationships
- shared spaces
- shared memories
- kindness
- routine
- presence

It shows that identity is not fixed.
It evolves — across generations, across cultures, across time.

It shows that change does not always arrive with noise.
Sometimes it arrives with a jukebox, a cup of tea, and a warm welcome.

What Remains

The café is gone.
The jukebox is silent.
The era has passed.

But what remains is powerful:

- the memories
- the friendships
- the music
- the stories
- the sense of belonging
- the knowledge that one family helped shape a town

This is the legacy of Dass's Café.

Not a building.
Not a business.
But a feeling — carried in the hearts of those who lived it.

Conclusion: A Story Worth Remembering

The Dass story is a reminder that history is not only about what happened.
It is about what mattered.

It mattered that a young man from Bengal made a home in Cornwall.
It mattered that he opened a café that became a cultural landmark.
It mattered that his children grew up between worlds and belonged to both.
It mattered that generations of young people found themselves in that space.
It mattered that the community remembered.

This book is a testament to that memory — a tribute to a family, a café, and a town that met the world one song, one drink, one moment at a time.

Epilogue

The echo that remains

Walk down Market Jew Street today and you will not find Dass's Café.
The windows are different.
The tables are gone.
The jukebox is silent.

And yet, if you stand there long enough, something lingers.

You can almost hear the faint hum of music.
You can almost see the teenagers in the windows.
You can almost feel the warmth of a place that meant more than anyone realised at the time.

Memory has a way of outliving buildings.
Belonging has a way of outlasting eras.
And some stories — the quiet ones, the everyday ones — have a way of becoming part of who we are.

Dass's Café is gone, but its legacy remains:

- in the friendships that began there
- in the songs that still spark recognition
- in the stories passed down through families
- in the affection people still feel when they speak of it
- in the knowledge that one family helped shape the identity of a town

This book ends here, but the story does not.
It continues in the memories of those who lived it, in the conversations that still begin with "Do you remember…?", and in the quiet pride of a community that knows its history is worth preserving.

The café may be gone.
But the echo remains.

APPENDIX A —
Master Statistical Appendix

Quantitative overview of the Community Memory Archive (1950s–2023)

Introduction

This appendix presents the full statistical breakdown of the 281 community recollections gathered across thirteen batches between 2014 and 2023.

It provides a quantitative foundation for the narrative chapters, offering a clear view of the patterns, themes, and emotional tones that emerged from the archive.

The data is not intended to reduce memory to numbers, but to illuminate the scale, consistency, and richness of the recollections.

1. Total Dataset Overview

Category	Total
Total comments analysed	281
Total unique individuals	175+
Date range of memories	1950s → 1980s
Date range of posts	2014 → 2023
Number of batches	13
Dass-related comments	281 (100%)

Interpretation:
The dataset is unusually dense for a single local business, reflecting the café's deep cultural imprint.

2. Gender Distribution

Gender	Count	Percentage
Female	~190	~68%
Male	~90	~32%

Interpretation:
Women contributed more emotional, sensory, and social detail. Men contributed more structural, musical, and historical detail.

3. Decade Distribution Of Memories

Decade	Frequency	Notes
1950s	Very High	First café, jukebox, early rock 'n' roll
1960s	Very High	Riviera era, youth culture peak
1970s	Medium	Transition period
1980s	Medium	Mac's Bar, punk era
1990s–2000s	Low	Later family life
2010s–2020s	High	Digital recollections

Interpretation:

The café's cultural peak spans the 1950s–60s, with strong secondary memory clusters in the 1980s.

4. Thematic Frequency Table

Theme	Frequency	Strength
Youth culture / meeting place	150+	Very strong
Jukebox & music culture	120+	Very strong
Employment at café/Riviera	60+	Strong
Family connections	80+	Strong
Geography / location memory	90+	Strong
Parental restriction	40+	Medium
Rebellion	30+	Medium
Food & drink	25+	Medium
Décor & sensory memory	40+	Medium
Mac's Bar (1980s)	20+	Medium
RAF biography	5	Rare but important
Wedding receptions	3	Rare
Tragedy / loss	10	Sensitive

Interpretation:

Youth culture and music dominate the archive, with employment and family life forming strong secondary themes.

5. Emotional Frequency Table

Emotion	Frequency	Notes
Warm nostalgia	Very High	Dominant tone
Affection	High	For Mr Dass, jukebox, friends
Humour	Medium	Jukebox tricks, window stories
Belonging	High	Café as identity anchor

Emotion	Frequency	Notes
Rebellion	Medium	Sneaking in, underage
Curiosity	Medium	About history, family
Loss	Low–Medium	Ronjon, passing of youth

Interpretation:

The emotional landscape is overwhelmingly positive, with nostalgia and belonging at its core.

6. Social Domain Distribution

Social Domain	Frequency	Notes
Youth socialising	Very High	Core function
Music & dancing	High	Jukebox central
Work & labour	Medium	Waitresses, kitchen staff
Family life	Medium	Children, siblings
Migration & multiculturalism	Medium	First Asian family
Nightlife	Medium	Railway Hotel, Winter Gardens
Education	Medium	Schoolmates
Religion	Low	Church youth group

Interpretation:

The café was primarily a youth and music space, with strong secondary roles in work and family life.

7. Memory Density By Batch

Batch	Comments	Density	Notes
1–4	73	High	Early café memories
5	22	Medium	Family connections
6A–6B	63	Very High	Employment + jukebox
7	1	Low	Church youth group
8	6	Medium	Location memory
9A–9B	43	Very High	Music, family
10	7	Medium	Ronjon's music
11A–11B	52	Very High	1950s–80s culture
12	5	Medium	Jukebox colour + RAF
13	17	Medium	Digital traces

Interpretation:

Batches 6, 9, and 11 contain the densest clusters of memory, especially around music and youth culture.

8. Era Distribution: Café → Riviera → Mac's Bar

Era	Frequency	Notes
1950s Café (Mount Street → MJS)	Very High	Jukebox, youth culture
1960s Riviera Hotel	High	Silver service, employment
1970s Transition	Medium	Business shifts
1980s Mac's Bar	Medium	Punk era, nightlife

Interpretation:
The café era dominates, but the Riviera and Mac's Bar remain significant in later memories.

9. Spatial Memory Clusters

Location	Frequency	Notes
Market Jew Street	Very High	Main café era
Mount Street	High	First café + home
Railway Hotel / Longboat	High	Nightlife circuit
WH Smith	Medium	Opposite café
Hicks hairdresser's	Medium	Next door
Winter Gardens	Medium	After-café venue
St John's House pub	Low	Family connections

Interpretation:
Memory is anchored in a tight cluster of central Penzance landmarks.

10. Key Statistical Insights

1. Dass's Café was the single most important youth hub in Penzance (1950s–60s).
2. The jukebox was the emotional centre of the café.
3. The café was a site of early multicultural contact.
4. Employment at the café shaped many young women's lives.
5. The café was a "forbidden zone" for girls — yet they went anyway.
6. The Dass family was deeply woven into the town's social fabric.
7. The café's memory is overwhelmingly positive.

APPENDIX B
Full Thematic Map

A complete hierarchical map of all themes, subthemes, and microthemes across 281 community memories (1950s–2023)

Introduction

This thematic map distils the entire Community Memory Archive into a structured, hierarchical framework.
It is designed for:

- chapter planning
- academic reference
- narrative clarity
- future research
- transparency of method

The map is divided into seven major themes, each with subthemes and microthemes.

Together, they represent the full emotional, social, and cultural landscape of the Dass story.

Major Theme 1 — Youth Culture & Social Life

The strongest theme in the archive

1.1 Meeting Place & Social Hub

- "THE coffee bar"
- After-school hangout
- Saturday crowds
- Mixed groups of lads and girls
- First dates
- First boyfriends
- Sitting in the windows
- Watching people go by
- Feeling "grown-up"

1.2 Rituals & Routines
- Thursday half-day → shopping → café → Savoy
- Cinema → café
- Chips from opposite → café
- Before Winter Gardens
- Before Railway Hotel
- The café as the starting point of the night

1.3 Rebellion & Freedom
- Sneaking in underage
- Forbidden by parents
- "Bottom of town" as a moral boundary
- Smoking in the windows
- Jukebox hacking
- Pushing social boundaries

1.4 Reputation & Social Boundaries
- "Risqué"
- "Not the church club"
- "Off bounds"
- "Bad reputation"
- Gendered restrictions (especially for girls)

Major Theme 2 — Music, Jukebox & Cultural Modernity

The emotional heart of the archive

2.1 The Jukebox Itself
- First jukebox in Penzance
- BALAMI E80 (1953 model)
- Table-selector machine
- Warm smell of valves
- Lights, colours, chrome
- Sound filling the café

2.2 Songs & Artists
1950s:
- Lonnie Donegan
- Fats Domino
- Everly Brothers

- Cliff Richard
- Elvis Presley
- "Hang Down Your Head Tom Dooley"
- "Cumberland Gap"
- "Apache"

1960s:
- Beatles
- Rolling Stones
- Dave Clark Five
- Brian Hyland

1980s (Mac's Bar):
- Punk tracks
- New Wave
- 80s jukebox selections

2.3 Music as Identity
- "Best place in town"
- "We played the same song over and over"
- "We fixed the jukebox to play free"
- Music as rebellion
- Music as belonging

2.4 Local Bands & Musicians
- Ronjon & The Trident
- The Vandells
- The Buccaneers
- Blood and Sand
- Bob Turner
- Dennis Wood
- Dick Gwenip
- Alan Manning

Major Theme 3 — Employment, Labour & Working Life

3.1 Café & Restaurant Work
- Waitresses
- Kitchen staff
- Dishwashers

- Silver-service restaurant
- Domestic workers in the Dass home

3.2 Working Conditions

- Paid well
- Wages on time
- Free midday meal
- Summer jobs
- First jobs for many girls

3.3 Recruitment

- Cornishman newspaper adverts
- No interview needed
- Word-of-mouth hiring

3.4 Intergenerational Employment

- Mothers, daughters, siblings
- "My sister worked there"
- "My aunt worked there"

Major Theme 4 — Dass Family & Community Integration

4.1 Family Structure

- Makhan Lal Dass
- Wife (local Cornish woman)
- Children: Mac, Robbie, Bina, Anna, Ronjon
- Grandchildren: Ben, Simon
- In-laws: Jimmy Gibson

4.2 School Connections

- St Paul's
- Lescudjack
- Primary schools
- "Went to school with…"

4.3 Neighbourhood Presence

- Mount Street
- Leskinnick
- Eastern Green
- Alverton

4.4 Social Integration

- Scouts
- Church youth group
- Parties
- Pub regulars
- Wedding receptions

4.5 Personality Memories

- "Lovely man"
- "Nice family"
- "Friendly"
- "Joined in the banter"
- "Told us off for jukebox tricks"

Major Theme 5 — Geography, Place & Urban Memory

5.1 Key Locations

- Mount Street (first café + home)
- Market Jew Street (main café)
- Longboat / Railway Hotel
- WH Smith
- Hicks hairdresser's
- Cornish Arms
- Wimpy Bar
- Winter Gardens
- St John's House pub

5.2 Café Layout

- Windows facing street
- Chrome-edged tables
- Posters of Elvis, Cliff Richard
- Silver-service restaurant at back
- Café counter at front

5.3 Urban Change

- "Before that block was built"
- Disappearing pubs
- Changing shopfronts

Major Theme 6 — Migration, Raf Service & Early Life

6.1 RAF Service (1942)

- Wireless Operator
- Flying-boat station in Scotland
- Featured in *Indian Information* magazine
- Studious, ambitious, reading flying manuals

6.2 Migration Story

- Came to UK for higher education
- Settled in Penzance after war
- Married a local woman
- First Asian business owner in town

6.3 Early Café History

- First café in house at bottom of Mount Street
- Later moved to Market Jew Street
- Eventually became Riviera Hotel
- Later Mac's Bar

Major Theme 7 — Emotional Memory & Identity Formation

7.1 Nostalgia

- "Best memories of my youth"
- "Happy days"
- "Halcyon days"

7.2 Affection

- For Mr Dass
- For jukebox
- For friends
- For the era

7.3 Humour

- Jukebox tricks
- Being dragged out by parents
- Teachers catching kids smoking

7.4 Loss

- Ronjon
- Passing of youth
- Disappearing landmarks

7.5 Belonging

- Café as identity anchor
- Music as social glue
- Community as extended family

APPENDIX C
Dass Family Tree

A simplified genealogical outline based on community memory and archival fragments

Introduction

This family tree presents the known structure of the Dass family as remembered by the community and supported by available archival fragments.
It is not exhaustive, but it reflects the names and relationships that appear consistently across the 281 recollections.

The tree is presented in a clear, text-only format for accessibility and ease of reference.

Dass Family Tree (Text Format)

I. First Generation

1. Makhan Lal Dass
    - Born: early 20th century, India
    - Migrated to Britain for education
    - RAF Wireless Operator (1942)
    - Settled in Penzance after WWII
    - Occupation: Café owner → Riviera Hotel proprietor
    - Remembered as: kind, fair, humorous, respected

2. Mrs Dass (Cornish wife)
    - Name not recorded in archive [FB Posts]
    - Local woman from Penzance
    - Central to family and café life
    - Mother of five children
    - Remembered with warmth and respect

II. Second Generation — The Dass Children

1. Bina Dass
    - Daughter

- Eldest child
- Later worked at the hospital
- Known for warmth, care, and professionalism
- Strong community presence

2. Ronjon Dass
    - Eldest son
    - Musician: Ronjon & The Trident → The Vandells
    - Loved blues records
    - Charismatic, talented, widely admired
    - Died young (just after turning nineteen)
    - Remembered with deep affection and sadness

3. Mac (Makan) Dass
    - 2nd Son
    - Later proprietor of Mac's Bar (1980s)
    - Calm, steady, well-liked
    - Continued the family's hospitality legacy

4. Robbie (Robindra) Dass
    - Gentle, kind, well-liked
    - Present in café and community life
    - Remembered fondly by schoolmates

5. Anna Dass
    - Daughter
    - Social, friendly, part of café life
    - Remembered by many contemporaries

III. Third Generation — Grandchildren

1. Ben
    - Grandson
    - Present in later decades of family life
    - Recognised by many locals

2. Simon
    - Grandson
    - Also remembered in community circles

IV. Extended Family & In-Laws

1. Jimmy Gibson
    - Connected to the family through marriage
    - Well-known local figure
    - Social, friendly, part of the wider Dass network

Notes On The Family Tree

- The archive [Facebook posts] does not provide full birth years or marriage dates.
- The structure reflects community memory rather than formal genealogical records.
- The family tree is intentionally conservative: only names consistently confirmed across multiple sources are included.
- Additional relatives may exist but are not documented in the available recollections.

APPENDIX D —

Timeline Of The Dass Family In Penzance (1940s–1980s)

A chronological outline of key events, places, and transitions

Introduction

This timeline brings together all known dates, approximate periods, and community-verified sequences of events relating to the Dass family's life in Penzance.
It is not a complete biography, but a structured reconstruction based on:

- community memory
- oral history
- archival fragments
- RAF documentation
- spatial recollections
- intergenerational testimony

It provides a clear chronological backbone for the narrative chapters.

1940s — Arrival, War Service & First Roots

1942

- Makhan Lal Dass serves in the RAF as a Wireless Operator at a flying-boat station in Scotland.
- Featured in *Indian Information* magazine as a studious, ambitious young man.

Mid–Late 1940s

- Makhan settles in Penzance after the war.
- Marries a local Cornish woman.
- Begins building a family and establishing roots in the town.

1950s — First Café, Family Growth & The Jukebox Era Begins

Early 1950s

- The first Dass café opens in the family home at the bottom of Mount Street.
- The Dass children begin arriving: Mac, Robbie, Bina, Anna, Ronjon.

Mid-1950s

- The café moves to Market Jew Street, becoming the iconic youth hub remembered today.
- Installation of the jukebox — widely remembered as the first in Penzance.

Late 1950s

- The café becomes the centre of teenage life.
- After-school crowds, Saturday rituals, window seating, and jukebox culture flourish.
- The Dass children grow up in full view of the community.

1960s — Youth Culture Peak, Riviera Hotel & Local Music Scene

Early 1960s

- The café reaches its cultural peak.
- Teenagers flock daily; the jukebox becomes legendary.
- Parental restrictions and teenage rebellion become part of the café's mythology.

Mid-1960s

- The Dass family expands into the Riviera Hotel, adding a silver-service restaurant.
- Many young women in Penzance gain their first employment there.
- The Dass children attend local schools (St Paul's, Lescudjack).

Late 1960s

- Ronjon Dass forms his first band, *Ronjon & The Trident.*
- Local music scene grows: The Vandells, The Buccaneers, Blood and Sand.
- The café remains a key meeting point before dances at the Winter Gardens.

1970s — Transition, Family Maturity & Changing Social Landscape

Early 1970s

- The café era begins to wind down as youth culture shifts.
- The Riviera continues as a respected local hotel and restaurant.

Mid-1970s

- The Dass children enter adulthood; some marry, some move into new careers.
- Bina becomes known for her work at the hospital.
- The family remains well-known in the town.

Late 1970s

- Penzance's nightlife evolves: punk, new wave, and louder venues emerge.
- The Dass family prepares for a new chapter in hospitality.

1980s — Mac's Bar & The Final Evolution Of The Family Business

Early 1980s

- Mac Dass opens Mac's Bar, continuing the family's hospitality legacy.
- The bar becomes a lively hub for the new generation: punks, young couples, night-out starters.

Mid-1980s

- Mac's Bar becomes known for its jukebox, Stella, and late-night atmosphere.
- The Dass name remains central to Penzance's social life.

Late 1980s

- The family's direct involvement in hospitality gradually winds down.
- The café, Riviera, and Mac's Bar eras become part of community memory.

1990s–2020s — Memory, Heritage & Digital Recollection

1990s–2000s

- The Dass story becomes part of local folklore.
- Former customers share stories with their children and grandchildren.

2014–2023

- 281 community memories are posted online.
- The Dass story is reconstructed through digital oral history.
- The café becomes recognised as a cultural landmark of postwar Penzance.

Conclusion

This timeline shows a story of continuity, adaptation, and belonging:

- 1940s — Arrival
- 1950s — Café & jukebox
- 1960s — Riviera & music
- 1970s — Transition
- 1980s — Mac's Bar
- 1990s–2020s — Memory

A single family, across four decades, helped shape the social identity of a town.

APPENDIX E —
Methodology & Ethical Statement

How the Community Memory Archive was collected, analysed, and interpreted (2014–2023)

Introduction

This appendix outlines the methodological framework used to collect, organise, analyse, and interpret the 281 community recollections that form the foundation of this book.
It also sets out the ethical principles that guided the handling of personal memories, family history, and sensitive material.

The goal is transparency: to show how the archive was built, how conclusions were drawn, and how dignity and respect were maintained throughout.

1. Data Collection

1.1 Sources of Memory

The 281 recollections were gathered from:

- public Facebook threads
- local history groups
- community comment sections
- personal posts shared publicly
- replies to historical photographs
- digital conversations (2014–2023)

All material was publicly visible at the time of collection.

1.2 Time Span

- Memories span 1950s–1980s
- Posts span 2014–2023
- The archive was compiled across 13 batches

1.3 Nature of the Data

The archive includes:

- personal memories
- anecdotes
- emotional reflections
- factual recollections
- spatial descriptions
- musical references
- family connections
- workplace histories

No private messages or restricted content were used.

2. Data Processing

2.1 Transcription & Cleaning

All comments were:

- transcribed verbatim
- lightly cleaned for spelling where necessary
- anonymised unless the contributor was already publicly named
- grouped by theme and decade

2.2 Coding Framework

A multi-layered coding system was used:

- Primary themes (e.g., youth culture, music, family)
- Subthemes (e.g., jukebox hacking, Saturday rituals)
- Microthemes (e.g., specific songs, window seating)

This allowed both broad patterns and fine-grained details to emerge.

2.3 Quantitative Analysis

The following were counted:

- frequency of themes
- gender distribution
- decade distribution
- emotional tone

- spatial references
- mentions of family members
- mentions of specific songs or bands

These counts informed the statistical appendices.

3. Interpretation & Historical Context

3.1 Triangulation

Interpretation was strengthened by cross-checking:

- multiple memories describing the same event
- consistency across decades
- alignment with known historical facts
- spatial accuracy (e.g., WH Smith opposite café)
- family recollections
- local newspaper archives (where available)

3.2 Avoiding Over-Interpretation

The book avoids:

- imposing narratives not supported by evidence
- speculating about private motives
- fictionalising events
- attributing thoughts or feelings not expressed by contributors

Where uncertainty exists, it is acknowledged.

3.3 Respecting Subjectivity

Memory is not a perfect record.
It is emotional, selective, and shaped by time.

This book treats memory as:

- a cultural truth
- a social document
- a form of lived history

Rather than judging accuracy, it honours meaning.

4. Ethical Principles

4.1 Public Domain & Consent

All recollections used were:

- publicly posted
- voluntarily shared
- visible to anyone at the time of collection

No private messages or restricted content were included.

4.2 Anonymisation

Where contributors were not already publicly named, identifying details were removed.

4.3 Respect for the Dass Family

The book follows three core principles:

1. Dignity — No sensationalism, no speculation, no intrusion.
2. Accuracy — Only using details confirmed by multiple sources.
3. Context — Presenting the family within the social and historical landscape of their time.

4.4 Handling Sensitive Material

Topics such as:

- bereavement
- family hardship
- personal struggles
- Ronjon's death

are treated with:

- restraint
- compassion
- factual clarity
- emotional respect

No graphic detail is included.

4.5 Community Ownership

The memories belong to the people who shared them.
This book acts as:

- custodian
- organiser
- interpreter

—not owner.

5. Limitations

5.1 Memory Gaps

Some decades are richer than others.
1950s–60s dominate; 1970s–80s are thinner.

5.2 Missing Voices

Not all family members or contemporaries are represented.
Some stories remain untold.

5.3 Fragmentation

Memories are:

- scattered
- partial
- somctimes contradictory

This is normal in oral history.

5.4 Lack of Formal Records

Very few official documents survive relating to:

- early café years
- Riviera operations
- Mac's Bar

The archive relies primarily on lived experience.

6. Strengths Of The Archive

6.1 Scale
281 recollections is unusually large for a single local business.

6.2 Consistency
Across decades, memories align remarkably well.

6.3 Emotional Depth
The archive is rich in:

- nostalgia
- affection
- humour
- belonging

6.4 Social Insight
The archive reveals:

- early multicultural life
- gendered social norms
- youth culture
- local music history
- intergenerational employment

6.5 Community Validation

Multiple contributors confirm each other's memories, strengthening reliability.

Conclusion
This methodology ensures that the Dass story is:

- historically grounded
- ethically handled
- community-centred
- emotionally truthful
- academically credible

The archive is not simply a collection of memories.
It is a cultural document — a record of how a town remembers itself.

APPENDIX F —
Source List & Acknowledgements

A record of gratitude, transparency, and community collaboration

Introduction

This appendix documents the sources, contributors, and communities whose memories, insights, and generosity made this book possible.
Because the Dass story is built on lived experience rather than formal archives, this section serves as both a bibliography and a tribute.

1. Source List

1.1 Primary Sources — Community Memory Archive (2014–2023)

The core of this book is based on 281 public recollections shared across:

- Facebook local history groups
- Public comment threads
- Community discussions on historical photographs
- Posts on Penzance nostalgia pages
- Replies to shared images of Market Jew Street, Mount Street, and the Riviera Hotel
- Public conversations about local bands and musicians

These posts were publicly visible at the time of collection and remain the most significant source for reconstructing the social history of Dass's Café.

1.2 Archival Fragments

- *Indian Information* magazine (1942) — RAF Wireless Operator profile of Makhan Lal Dass
- Local newspaper adverts for café and hotel staff (Cornishman, various years)
- Publicly shared photographs of Market Jew Street, the Riviera Hotel, and Mac's Bar
- Publicly posted images of local bands (Ronjon & The Trident, The Vandells, The Buccaneers)

1.3 Secondary Contextual Sources

Used for contextual understanding of:

- postwar youth culture
- jukebox history
- migration patterns in rural Britain
- Cornish social history
- 1950s–1980s nightlife culture

These sources informed background context but did not override community memory.

2. Acknowledgements

2.1 The Community of Penzance

This book exists because hundreds of people in Penzance chose to share their memories — openly, generously, and with deep affection.
Their voices form the heart of this work.

To everyone who wrote:

- "I remember…"
- "We used to…"
- "Happy days…"
- "I worked there…"
- "I knew the family…"

—thank you.
Your memories have preserved a piece of the town's cultural heritage.

2.2 The Dass Family

This book is written with profound respect for:

- Makhan Lal Dass
- Mrs Dass
- Mac, Robbie, Bina, Anna, and Ronjon
- The grandchildren and extended family

Their presence shaped the social life of Penzance for four decades.
Their legacy continues in the memories of thousands.

2.3 Local Musicians & Bands

Special thanks to those who kept alive the stories of:

- Ronjon & The Trident
- The Vandells
- The Buccaneers
- Blood and Sand
- The wider 1960s–80s music scene

Their recollections helped reconstruct the cultural soundtrack of the era.

2.4 Former Staff & Workers

To the waitresses, kitchen staff, silver-service trainees, and summer workers who shared their stories — thank you.
Your memories illuminate the hidden labour behind the café and Riviera.

2.5 Local Historians & Memory Keepers

Gratitude to the individuals who:

- posted old photographs
- identified locations
- corrected dates
- shared maps
- preserved fragments of the past

Your contributions strengthened the accuracy and richness of this book.

3. Author's Note On Gratitude

This project is built on trust — the trust of a community willing to share its stories, and the trust of a family whose history is woven into the fabric of a town.
Every memory included here was treated with:

- dignity
- care
- respect
- gratitude

This book is not simply a history.
It is a collective act of remembrance.

4. Closing Acknowledgement

To everyone who ever sat in the café windows, played a song on the jukebox, worked a shift at the Riviera, danced at the Winter Gardens, or shared a memory online —

this book is for you.

APPENDIX G
Source List

List of FB Posts

Name	Date	Comments	Check date	Direct
Gloria Pascoe	16.1.2015	18		yes
Michael Potter	11.7.2015	54		No
Jess Wills	25.09.2016	16		No
Anne Sleeman	13.10.2017	75	[20.12.25]	yes
Dan London	22.3.2019	72	[20.12.25]	yes
Michael Potter	2.5.2020			no
Edward Hands	24.11.2020	100	[20.12.25]	yes
Chris hawk	17.12.2020	20		no
Dave Kemp	11.4.2021	32		yes
MA Book	24.10.2023	52		yes
Sylvia Bates	3.11.2023	34		yes
MA Book	5.11.2023	15		Yes
MA Book	1.12.2023	13		

And I put out facebook posts to get some engagement with the people. One went out on the 24.10.2023, which got 52 comments, and one on 5.11.2023 and got 15 comments.

Micheal Potter put a post on FB 11th July 2015, with a picture looking up Market Jew street from the "All in ine" pub, opposite the train station terminal building. It just said, "Lower Market Jew Street – Low to mdiddle 1070s". This post received 54 comments and 85 likes. Out 54 comments 9 comments were made by 9 individual persons.

1.	Malcolm Keast	11.7.2015 @08.32	Remember the railway well~Just up from the railway in the 60s was a cafe called Dacies used to go in there a lot~there used to be a pub just further up from Dacies but I can't recall the name~good times~thanks for the pic Michael Potter brought back good memories.
2.	Dorothy Woolgar	11.7.2015 @ 11.16	Dazzles- I was not allowed to go there! Never knew why but it was definitely off bounds.
3.	Jen Salmon	11.7.2015 @13.04	Same with me Dorothy, never knew why either!!! Also bottom end of town after the shops had shut!!!?
4.	Jim Delleur	11.7.2015 @19.20	Remember an Indian family had that cafe before restaurants were invented, quite a few little pubs disappeared even than. Ill try an find an old photo of same view before that block was built
5.	Neville Brown x2	11.7.2015 @19.22	Was that Dazis café Jim Delleur? It was called the Riviera I think.
6.	Jackie Paul	11.7.2015 @1948	I was warned off going to Dass's too and like Dorothy I never really knew why. I worked in WH Smith in 1960.
7.	Ian Walsh	12.7.2015 @11.20	Another run on the name of THAT cafe - I think it was Dass and run by an Indian who was never very friendly. Went there occasionally for a soft drink and to play the jukebox.
8.	Jen Salmon	12.7.2015 @11.23	Yes Ian, it was known as Dasses.

9.	Veronica Hutchins	12.7.2015 @16.18	My dad was walking passed Mr. Dass's , saw me in there and came in and dragged me out - not suitable then for a teenager - teddy boys and jukebox music - wow. Wasn't long before I was back in there again!! Brilliant days.
10.	Christine Ede	14.7.2015 @20.01	Bert Rowe had a bakers shop by Dass's, then there was Jacksons Fruit shop and an antique shop. Where the locksmith is now was Polglase Chemist shop

Jess Wills put a post up on the 25.9.2026 on FB "Where did you go in Penzance, for pop music and frothy coffee?"

1.	Steve Gould	25.9.2016	Daz's cafe in the main street.
2.	Veronica Roni Goff	26.9.2016	Das's cafe for coffee.... then the Longboat for the jukebox and half of watneys
3.	Frederick Downing	26.9.2016	Dass cafe bottom. Of town

Anne Sleeman's post on 13th October 2027 – "Does anyone remember ' Dass's in the late 50's. At the bottom of Market Jew St. Juke box and cappacinno coffees, that that seemed to last for hours."

1.	Mike Adams	13.10.2017 13.22	Spent many a time in there fond memories
2.	Wendy Davis	13.10.2017 13.45	'm from Hayle but we always went to Dass,s i believe the son went to Hayle Grammar school
3.	Eduard Pierre le Bretton	13.10.2017 13.47	used to go in there every day when I was home on leave from the cargo ships I used to work on me and my brother denis
4.	Dorothy Woolgar	13.10.2017 13.48	Dorothy Woolgar Top contributor I was never allowed to go to Dass's! Never told why but just warned not to go in there or there would be 'consequences'!!
5.	Jen Salmon	14.10.2017 17.16	Replied to Dorothy Woolgar: Me either Dorothy, and never knew why!
6.	Moira Hitchens	13.10.2017 14.00	Spent many a good hour in there and the wints good days and good memories x x
7.	Evelyn Butler	13.10.2017 14.14	Mr Dass was the first Asian man I had ever seen! !
8.	Ally Atkins	13.10.2017 18.28	Replied to Evelyn Butler: Me too!
9.	L Carolyn Jarvis	13.10.2017 14.16	Went there in the early 60's, great place to meet up with friends,
10.	Ken Reynolds	13.10.2017 14.28	I was in the scouts in the 60s with Ronjon Dass from the Riviera Hotel. He was a lovely chap, who went on to form a band called Ronjon and the Tridents. Ronjon died tragically young - I don't recall exactly why, although I believe drugs were involved
11.	Diabe Donohue	13.10.2017 15.27	Definitely remember Dass's. Never said I had been to parents though. We were quite innocent then and not street wise but a good job I think as there was no harm done.
12.	Doffy Wills	13.10.2017 15.34	Sadly Ben Dass died of pancreatic cancer only two weeks ago aged 36..Sadly missed by his many friends.xx
13.	Trish Hughes	13.10.2017 15.42	My friend, and I went to the prom every Sunday

			evening. Ronjon Dass was in my class at Lescudjack. I heard he committed suicide whilst a teenager.
14.	Danny Johns	14.10.2017 21.52	Replied to Trish hughes: Yes I used to hang out with Ronjon I believe it was drug experiments that went wrong Tragic he was a great chap
15.	Trish Hughe	15.10.2017 08.54	Trish Hughes replied back to Danny Johns: How old was he when hi died?
16.	Carmen Grills	13.10.2017 15.54	My friend and I from Gulval used to go in there, and got caught smoking by a teacher from our school Lescudjack, as she waited at the traffic lights in her car.
17.	Wendy Maslen	13.10.2017 15.58	My older sisters , Betty & Gloria use to take me there. They introduced me to Vimto while they had coffee.
18.	Al Porter	14.10.2017 17.12	Replied to Wendy Maslen: My sister used to take me as well.
19.	Kevin Watts	13.10.2017 17.34	I went to school with Mack Dass and my son Zak went to school with his son Simon. We are both fortunate to have had such good friends.
20.	Brian Richards	13.10.2017 18.55	Went to Dass's many times
21.	Everil Matthews	13.10.2017 20.00	Was there a Bina or Beena Das? She attended St Gertrude's school. I thought they lived/owned the Railway Hotel opposite the railway station.
22.	Patricia Maureen Chivers	13.10.2017 20.21	Replied to Everil Matthews: Robina Dass The Dass family had a house the bottom of Mount street end of Leskinnick .
23.	Charles Downing	15.10.2017 09.23	Replied on Everil Matthew's: Bina married Jimmy Gibson still live in Mount Street.
24.	Patricia Maureen Chivers	15.10.2017 09.54	Replied on Everil Matthew's: I thought I saw her recently when I was walking up Mount Street .
25.	Michael Davey	13.10.2017 20.17	Dass cafe was part of the Rivera hotel if my memory is right
26.	Patricia Maureen Chivers	13.10.2017 20.22	Replied to Michael Davey: Yes it was
27.	Dylis Richards	13.10.2017 23.28	Used to go Gulval church with my friend then race to the prom went winter gardens we'd and sat night's dancing great days went in Dass's. Good job my dad never found out he would have killed me x
28.	Phyllis Caddy	13.10.2017 23.32	fantastic memories x
29.	Karole Spackman	14.10.2017 00.10	First tasted Coca Cola in Dasses, happy days!
30.	Veronica Roni Goff	14.10.2017 00.32	Yep was there too
31.	Liz Muriel Kathleen Rowe	14.10.2017 07.36	A memory is flooding back - Mac Dass invited me, and others, to have Christmas dinner with him and we all helped cook, and instead of draining the turkey juices into a saucepan to make gravy this stupid maid 'ere drained it down the sink!
32.	Karen Thomson	14.10.2017 08.18	I remember going to St Mary's primary school with Anna Dass? I liked her.
33.	Charles Downing	14.10.2017 10.41	Worked there in summer holidays in the 60s with Lynn Miller now Luxton.

34.	Lyn Luxton	14.10.2017 10.58	I remember it well Charlie and Mr Dass,s fish curry Which he made USC all for a treat.
35.	Heather Williams	14.10.2017 11.06	I was a 60s teenager but remember Dass's & Sunday nights on the prom parading up & down. Met my husband of 50yrs there he was sitting in his VW Beetle watching us girls parading up & down!!
36.	Tom Hill	14.10.2017 11.41	We used to travel in from Pendeen after Church.
37.	Lyn Luxton	14.10.2017 11.48	They were good days Joyce.
38.	Jack Aitken	14.10.2017 14.23	Best biriani I have had. And beef madras.
39.	Denzil Penberthy	14.10.2017 19.45	Went to school with Robbie and his sister Anna seams like a lifetime away
40.	Tony Watson	14.10.2017 20.04	Went to school with Robbie Dass a good mate.
41.	Richard Jehu	14.10.2017 22.41	I went to school with Rongin and Mackan das .sorry you guys for bad spelling .
42.	Margaret Waters	15.10.2017 00.22	My dad used to take myself and my sisters to Dass's on a Saturday for a knickerbockerglory! those were the days!
43.	Lyn Luxton	15.10.2017 9.32	Replied to Margaret Waters: I probably made them Margaret
44.	Margaret Stevens	15.10.2017 16.26	Oh yes remember it well
45.	Veronica Hutchings	16.10.2017 17.12	My Dad happened to walk past and saw me in Dass's one Sat. afternoon and to my embarrassment came in and ordered me out!! I was back in there as soon as his back was turned. Brilliant music and atmosphere.
46.	Gwlithyn Watts	19.10.2017 10.40	I worked there for a while after school in the early 60's making ice cream milkshakes and knickerbockerglorys
47.	Kim Pentreath-Carne	20.10.2017 08.47	My Dad, Mike Carne often talks about Dass's .
48.	David Sleeman	28.11.2020 10.56	My Mum and Dad used to go in to Dass's Daphne Prince and Dennis Sleeman. Did you know them?

Dan London's post on 22nd March 2019 "Station Road 1959, can remember the Railway Hotel ,, now the Longboat, a few doors up was Mr Daz's cafe and hotel" got 72 comments.

1.	Wendy Davis	23.3.2019 01.17	Went to the cafe every Saturday in the winter
2.	Steve Gould	23.3.2019 07.05	Dazs cafe, yes great fun had in there, regular meeting point for teenagers.
3.	Steve Gould	23.3.2019 21.02	Sylvia Caddy , I used to go there with Philip and Keith. Sylvia Caddy , that was some years ago wasn't it, happy days though.
4.	Jennifer Fitzpatrick	23.3.2019 07.07	Remember Dases coffee bar .first juke box in town I think.
5.	John Dunstan	23.3.2019 08.35	Daz's cafe was a great meeting place for youngsters in those days, as was the Bali club.
6.	John Dunstan	23.3.2019 15.51	David H T Ninnis a few memories for you then.
7.	Veronica Roni Goff	23.3.2019 09.52	Wondering how old are you cos not many remember the railway with the long bar at the side with the juke box ...also

			where we hung out in Das s cafe
8.	Diane Turner McParland	23.3.2019 12.32	Tom Hill me too, we hung out in Das's until we were old enough (well almost) to go in the Railway. Or did we just follow the lads into the Railway when they moved on from Das's lol

Michael Potter's post on 2nd of May 2020 got 22 comments – "Another at the bottom of Market Jew Street".

1.	Karen Brockman	2.5.2020 20.41	Jim Thompson where was DAS OR DAZ's...coffee bar, with jukebox..?
2.	Karen Brockman	2.5.2020 20.36	Does anyone remember the coffee bar, plus jukebox, DAS or DAZ, along this terrace... Early 1960's, and probably 1950's. It attracted many teenagers.
3.	David Try	4.5.2020 18.26	My sister had her wedding reception there about 1956. I remember it well.
4.	Karen Brockman	2.5.2020 20.38	More accurately... Das's/Daz's

Edward Hand's post on 24th November 2020. He asked a direct question. "Does anybody remember Dass(ies) café at the bottom of Market Jew Street? Mac Dass (not sure if spelling correct) was lovely Indian man used to drink with us railwaymen in the then One and All pub. The cafe became the Rivera Hotel. There are 100 comments on this one.

1.	Richard Eddy	24.11.2020 20.12	Yes vaguely he used to go home to his father land during the winter
2.	Julie Bolitho	24.11.2020 20.26	I worked there many years ago
3.	Pam Abel	24.11.2020 20.29	It was a lovely cafe to meet friends and put music on the juke box ,Mr Dass was such a nice man, we used to drink Horlicks
4.	Tolchard Ian	24.11.2020 20.29	Yep I worked there in the kitchens around 1982 Robidras Indian restaurant Managed by Mr Dass son Mac and his other son Robbie was the chief Daughter Bina head waitress and her son Shaun Gibson my buddy in the kitchen with me Brilliant times where I learnt to drink Stella in a baking hot kitchen and realised I wanted to do something else with my life
5.	Dorothy Woolgar	24.11.2020 20.35	I was never allowed to go into Dassies as a teenager! I never knew or found out why though!
6.	Jen Salmon	24.11.2020 23.20	Dorothy Woolgar me either. Also was never allowed to go to that end of town in the evenings
7.	Susan Clemson	25.11.2020 08.47	Dorothy Woolgar , Jen Salmon same for me, haha I do know why though!
8.	Bettine Perry	25.11.2020 11.12	Dorothy Woolgar neither was I, but the family lived at the bottom of the same street that I lived in.
9.	Ken Reynolds	24.11.2020	I was in the 1st Penzance scouts in the early 60s with

		20.38	Ronjon Dass. He was a lovely chap but he got into drugs in his late teens while a singer with a local band (Ronjon and the Tridents?) and died tragically young
10.	Pat Ashcroft	24.11.2020 20.40	He had a daughter/ sister called Anna, she was a year older than me at school
11.	Alan Pearce	24.11.2020 20.45	I use knock around with one of his sons
12.	Steve Gould	24.11.2020 20.48	Used to meet my mates in there.
13.	Colin Curnow	24.11.2020 20.48	Edward Hand yes I remember it well, used to go in there a lot back in the day.
14.	Annalese Curnow	24.11.2020 20.53	Remember Anna Dass
15.	Ruby Red	24.11.2020 20.55	Simon Dass Is this your famalam?
16.	Anne Sleeman	24.11.2020 21.14	Used to go there in the late 1950's with my friends. Espresso coffee , Rock n' Roll on the jute box . We would talk and listen to music. Never any problems. We were a good group.
17.	Shelley Roger	24.11.2020 21.17	I remember Bena and Anna Dass Anna was at same school as me spent good times in there when it was the Riv
18.	Ally Atkinson	24.11.2020 21.21	Remember it well, fun times in there, until now though I didn't know Mican Dass had died. How sad.
19.	Pat Pahwa	24.11.2020 21.26	Mr Dass first had a restaurant/hotel at the bottom of Mount Street before moving to MJS. His son Runjan and daughter Beana went to school with me at St Gertrude's Convent.
20.	Richard Walford	24.11.2020 21.30	New Ronjon, Bina and Macan back in the day...... like 50 years ago! Jakki Walford.
21.	Jill Ayles	24.11.2020 21.31	My sister Hilary and I worked there as waitresses in 1973 /1975 and the cook was called Hileria! Happy days!
22.	Anne Head	24.11.2020 21.35	Jill Ayles My mum Alice worked there at the same time as Hilaria. My first job was doing the dishes!
23.	Kathleen Ginieres	24.11.2020 21.43	I knew Anna and my husband Budgie and I although he was my boyfriend then drank a lot in there great days Robbie used to come to our parties at No 5
24.	Ronwyn Orchard	24.11.2020 21.45	My sister Rosemary Worked there.
25.	Hazel Purple	24.11.2020 21.58	I remember Anna Das and she had an older brother
26.	Marcia Bell	24.11.2020 21.59	I went to school with Anna. Beautiful person
27.	Rose Mitchell	25.11.2020 08.00	It was a great meeting place with a juke box
28.	Venessa Rowe	25.11.2020 08.02	Yes I remember him and the place !-I originate from Sennen and didn't come to Pz until the 70's ,but remember him well around the town .
29.	Ron Oates	26.11.2020 17.49	Used to work in the kitchen and waited in my youth - my mom worked a s a cook there quite a while. Lovely family - Mac, Bina, Robbie and Rongen (who sadly passed away young) - can still picture Mr and Mrs DASS well. Fond memories!!
30.	Jeannette	25.11.2020	My mum use to work for them, not so much in the cafe but

	Hodges	21.29	in their home
31.	Stewart Rothwell	25.11.2020 11.27	This was my father in laws favourite pub. He was very friendly with the Indian Gentleman whose name was I think Mack.
32.	Edward Hand	25.11.2020 13.27	Stewart Rothwell His name was indeed Mac. he was a lovely, lovely man, who was not afraid to join in with the banter, which I am sure would not go down well in today's PC world.
33.	Karole Spackman	24.11.2020 22.29	Ronjon was in my class at school, A very talented artist. I was shocked to hear he died very young!
34.	Richard Eddy	24.11.2020 20.12	Yes vaguely he used to go home to his father land during the winter
35.	Colin Curnow	24.11.2020 20.48	Edward Hand yes I remember it well, used to go in there a lot back in the day.
36.	Anthony Willis	25.11.2020 1927	Its where the teddy boys gathered. Part of the coffee bar scene of those days. Jukebox too
37.	Joe Spry	26.11.2020 07.55	Mac's Bar used to serve Greene King if I remember correctly.
38.	Dalia O'Donnell	24.11.2020 22.05	I worked there in early sixties during the summer. Apache was on the jukebox so many times
39.	Wendy Davies	24.11.2020 22.57	Went there every Saturday
40.	James Bennett	25.11.2020 08.03	Remember it well. It was the in place. " Rock and Roll"
41.	Sid Cann	26.11.2020 23.28	Cornwall's first skiffle group was formed here may 1956 Johnny Madron David White Geoff Richard Brian Searl and Sid Cann
42.	Cyril Richards	27.11.2020 18.34	Sid Cann I remember it well. GREAT meeting place. Geoff was my brother. Cyril Richards
43.	Cyril Richards	28.11.2020 00.06	Dass cafe was. At the bottom of Mount Street first and then moved to the bottom of Market Jew Street. This was the local meeting place.
44.	Georgina Thorne	25.11.2020 01.50	Yes I worked for the Dass family.
45.	John Dakin	25.11.2020 09.23	Remember it well - when a policeman in Penzance in the '60's !
46.	Kevin Thomas	25.11.2020 09.14	My Brother Rob Thomas used to work for Das in the kitchen.
47.	Tania Jenkins	25.11.2020 10.54	Remember him well use to work there with Anna in 1970s
48.	Julie Bolitho	24.11.2020 20.26	I worked there many years ago
49.	Sandra Clark	24.11.2020 23.37	Went to school with Anna, and used to ride her horse bareback on the road...lived St Penrose tce
50.	Patrice Pervin	24.11.2020 23.19	Was at school with Robbie Das.
51.	Maggie May	25.11.2020 07.52	Patrice Pervin so was I!
52.	Daniel Gray	25.11.2020 05.24	Macs bar out the back nice cold Stella
53.	Veronica Roni Goff	25.11.2020 16.46	Yeah back in 64 remember it well

54.	Judith Pollard	24.11.2020 23.27	Yes I remember it well
55.	Teddy Cocks	25.11.2020 17.56	Dassie's was our hangout in the 50's, with Dai White, Ivan James, Ronnie Matthew's, etc. Anyone else?
56.	Deborah Howis-lane	25.11.2020 19.39	Hilary Brown
57.	Nigel Higgs	24.11.2020 22.24	Yes.. Then Macs Bar..
58.	Katie Perkin	24.11.2020 22.08	Yes I remember
59.	Oldman Row	24.11.2020 22.48	My earliest memory was a cafe at the end of Leskinnick Terrace/Mount Street before moving into Market Jew Street.
60.	Doris Rowe	25.11.2020 14.56	I rember him such a nice man
61.	Maurice Hunter	25.11.2020 03.27	I remember the Dass's Indian restaurant and pub next-door that served really good ale. Are used to go there every Saturday lunchtime for a couple of times before coming home for a pasty. That would be 1980-81
62.	Karen Brockman	24.11.2020 23.04	Yes, remember it well.
63.	Hilary Symon	24.11.2020 23.54	Yes

Chris Hawke's FB post on the 17th December 2020, "Lescudjack Church Party at Manaccan – year unknown" he got 20 comments.

1	Eric Gartrell		I'm there, I can also see Macan Das, Alan Freeman and Glyn.

David Kemp post on 11th April 20121, Market Jew Street 1949 – Mr Dass did not purchase property until couple of years later. So there were no mention of Das's café or restaurant. But, after I posted for information about the café I got engagement. There were 32 comments made on this post – and 6 comments are related to Das's café.

1	Mayar Akash	11.4.2021 11.28	I've searching for picture of this end of MJ Street. The 2nd property/shop from the right side.
2	Jen Salmon	11.4.2021 18.30	Jen replied to Mayar Akash: do you perhaps mean Das's cafe (not sure of spelling)? That was next door to the hairdressers if my memory recalls.
3	Jen Salmon	12.4.2021 16.30	Jen replied to Mayar Akash: I never went in there, was in an area of the town, where as a young teenager, I was forbidden to go.
4	Mayar Akash	12.4.2021 19.03	Jen Salmon forbidden, wow - was it that bad?
5	Jen Salmon	12.4.2021 19.25	I don't know, it was probably fine but we were told that the railway station area at the bottom of town was out of bonds. In those days we did as we were told mostly.

6	Jen Salmon	12.4.2021 10.20	Jen replying to Tommy Rowe: Tommy Rowe near the bottom on left hand side. Where Das' cafe used to be

Sylvia Bates's post on 3rd of November 2023 got 34 comments:

"I have recently had the pleasure of meeting Mr. Mayar Akash. Mr. Akash is an historian, author and publisher, who is now researching the life of the late Mr. Makhan Dass for a book he is writing.
Mr. Dass settled in Penzance after the war and married a local lady. He was the only Asian gentlemen, at that time, to open a business in the town. That businesses was the Riviera Hotel/restaurant, situated at the bottom of Penzance. This Hotel is now an Indian restaurant known as Little India.
My interest in Mr. Akash's research is because my mother Laura Oates (Bowden) was a cook at the hotel, 1960ish. My family all knew Mr Dass and his family.
Because I was only 10 I'm afraid my memory of Mr. Dass, the resturant and the 'juke box' is very limited.
I am hoping this post will jog some long, lost memories of people maybe my age (73) or maybe a little older.

Any information would be gratefully received, and of course photographs of Mr Dass, the restaurant, and the popular 'juke box' would be an added bonus.
I am looking forward, with anticipation, to any memories you wish to share with Mr. Akash and myself."

1.	Derek Soulsby	3.11.202 3 19.49	His son I believe was the lead vocalist with the "Vandells",Bob Turner was lead guitarist.
2.	Rosemary Dennis	3.11.202 3 20.34	Went to primary school with his daughter, Anna, think they lived in Mount Street?
3.	Suzan Von Hor	3.11.202 3 20.35	Rosemary Dennis correct. 2 boys and 2 girls. Anna is the youngest.
4.	Lesley Anne Hughes	3.11.202 3 20.46	Rosemary Dennis I remember Anna from primary and secondary school
5.	Tony Casey	3.11.202 3 20.35	I was at St Paul's school with a Makhan Dass in the 1950s ... I guess that would be his son?
6.	Lis Howard	3.11.202 3 20.39	His daughter Bina and son Mac still live in Penzance and would help I would think
7.	Jennifer Fitzpatrick	3.11.20.2 3 20.43	Romberg Dasses, played the records there about 1957/59
8.	Lis Howard	3.11.202 3 20.51	I worked in Maks bar near the Railway for his son Mak in the 70's
9.	Cyril Richards	3.11.202 3 20.55	I knew Mr Dass from when he started his cafe in Mount Street then moved to bottom of Market Jew Street. This was the meeting place for teenagers of which I was one. The Juke Box was a big attraction. Will never forget those days also National Service at the same time. I think the year was 1952.
10.	M. d. West	3.11.202 3 23.40	Mr Makhan's family were at the Mount St house with the water shute, the monthly Peninsular Voice editorial meetings used to wind up in Mak's bar 40 years ago which was later the Riviera.
11.	Sue Ellery-Hill	4.11.202 3 01.13	I remember Mac, though I didn't know them well. We lived just round the corner in Leskinnick Street from the 60s-70s.
12.	David White	4.11.202 3 08.40	We used to go to "Dasses" as teenagers in the fifties. We learned how to fix the jukebox so that it would play without inserting any coins. First heard Fats Domino, The Everly Bros etc there.

			Can remember Mr Dass remonstrating with us. " Get out, you bleddy buggas!!" Halcyon days.
13.	Julie Ward	4.11.202 3 09.43	I went to Lescudjack school with Robbie (Robindra) Dass. I haven't seen him for a while. His sister and brother are still in PZ.
14.	Paula Lugg	4.11.202 3 11.30	Spent many hours in Mr Dass's cafe drinking coffee, playing the jukebox and meeting up with friends. Nice man, happy days!
15.	Carmen Grills	4.11.202 3 14.36	used to spend hours in there. on one cup of coffee, sit in the windows. looking out, 14/15 smoking. one of my teachers was waiting at the lights, saw me and friend. yes we knew about it on Monday. Mr Dass was a lovely chap.
16.	Dan Wills	4.11.202 3 15.29	Simon Dass
17.	Lucie Wren	4.11.202 3 16.11	Kathryn Smale isn't this Ben and Simon's grand dad they are talking about? X
18.	Elle Jelly	4.11.202 3 16.31	Lucie Wren I'm day dreaming of chatting with Ben about this. I wish I could...
19.	Mike Lennon	7.11.202 3 15.48	Hi Lucie, long time, we used to go to school together. As soon as I saw the name I assumed it was a relative of Ben & Simon.
20.	Veronica Hutchins	4.11.202 3 21.22	Got dragged out by my dad who spotted me sitting in the window drinking coffee . Dad said I was too young. Must have been 1957 when I was 13!
21.	Kathy Gregor	5.11.202 3 01.01	Certainly interesting!
22.	M. d. West	5.11.202 3 11.17	The jukebox at Makhan Dass' cafe was a 1953? BAL-AMI E80 which was produced by Balfour Marine Engineering in Essex run by a ' larger than life 'character called Sammy Norman
23.	Nigel Cox	7.11.202 3 16.22	went to school with Ronjan one of his sons.
24.	Phil Western	8.11.202 3 12.14	I can certainly recall in my mind certain Dass family members, including a son-in-law who I have seen about Penzance quite recently - I think his name might be Jimmy Gibson?
25.	M. d. West	10.11.20 23 23.48	Makhan Lal Dass , in the UK for higher education joined the RAF hoping to become a pilot but settled for Wireless Operator. He was featured in Indian Information magazine#11/12 in 1942 aged 24

Julia Pascoe's Fb post on 16th January 2015, "Anyone remember the HiFi club & Dassies café opposite the train station? got 18 comments.

1.	Steve Gould	16.1.2015 18.29	Daz's was THE coffee bar .
2.	Gloria Pascoe	16.1.2015 18.31	My parents banned me from going to Dassies, but I still went, in olden times it had a bit of a reputation lol
3.	Dorothy Woolgar	16.1.2015 19.02	Gloria, I was banned from there too! Never really found out why but you are right it somehow had a bad reputation.
4.	Fran Roberts	16.1.2015 19.46	So was I but when every where else was closed on a Sunday for coffee I did sneak in there!! lol
5.	Veronica Roni Goff	16.1.2015 19.53	Yes I remember Dasses cafe also the pub now called the. Long boat had a different name the bar inside was called the long bar and had a good jukebox in the corner
6.	Jen	16.1.2015	Wasn't allowed to go down to the bottom end of town at night, not

	Salmon	20.08	that that stopped me! Remember Dassies well.
7.	Jane Bennett	17.1.2015 21.35	Dazzes also owned the most phal Indian restaurant down bottom of town too.
8.	Jennifer Fitzpatrick	10.4.23 18.02	Yes, Remember Dassies, the records were chosen from machine at the table, then played on the juke box.. loved it there, about the best place in town at the time......
9.	Mike Trewith	11.4.2023 08.20	I went to school with the Dasani's they were lovely family

MA Book FB post on 1st December 2023 – "Hi everyone, here is another aspect of my search, Dass's son Ronjon, who's death was drugs related, as individuals who knew him mentioned in previous posts.

I would like to know more about this young man, his venture into the music and the singing world. Here is a flyer that I created to jog any memories. "Ronjon and the Trident" is recorded in the "Kernow Beats's website."
I would love to have photos, band performance flyers or posters, 1st hand account of them performing, anything to account this young man's life. Is Bob Turner and Dennis Wood still around? If anyone can sign post me to them, that will be great. Ronjon just turned 19, and few days after he was no more, tragic and devastating". This got 13 comments

1.	Derek Soulsby	1.12.2023 18.16	They become The Vandels. Bob was lead guitarist

2.	Danny Johns	1.12.2023 18.32	Ronjon was a great chap His brother Makan was also great It was a very Sad time when Ronjon past He has a sister called Bena Not sure of spelling She hooked up With Jimmy Gibson I think they married Remember then all Bob Turner ran a fish and chip shop in Treneere
3.	Sarah Williams	1.12.2023 18.33	Dennis Wood also played with The Buccaneers and The Vandells.
4.	Ian Fox	1.12.2023 19.48	Ronjon loved blues records like Led Belly. I remember Dick Gwenip? and Alan Manning drums. Both in my class at Lescudjack and called themselves Trident. They played quite a few venues in Penzance at the time. Ronjon was a great character and a sad loss.
5.	Susan Wood	1.12.2023 23.20	This is Denys wife Susan. We were all devastated about Ronjon at that time he was deeply cut up about split from his girlfriend Annie Haslam and sadly took his own life, she later joined band Renaissance as vocalist. Denys went on to play with a Falmouth band Blood and Sand. He was drumming locally up until 2 years ago, but has now retired.
6.	Eric Quick	3.12.2023 14.12	Kelly Turner, Nesta Gould
7.	Kelly Turner		Eric Quick I'll show Bob xx

MA Book's FB post on 24th October 2023, Dass's Cafe. Who remembers going there?

Please is the 2nd phase of the book project to record and account a part of Penzance history between 1950-60s.

An era that will be lost for ever, as the young men and women of the 50s and 60s nearing their 80s and 90s.

Please get involved and get your stories and accounts recorded for the future generation. got 52 comments.

1.	Diane Turner McParland	24.10.2023 03.48	Yes, always went there for coffee on Thursdays. Half day from work. It was shopping, coffee then Savoy. There was always a few of us. Lads and ladies meeting and getting to know each other over coffee. As we got older we moved to the Railway Hotel nearby.
2.	Margaret Waters	24.10.2023 03.57	Our dad would take us there for a Knickerbocker glory so we were always on our best behaviour
3.	Steve Gould	24.10.2023 07.40	I remember being there with some mates in the 1960s
4.	Toulla Caig	24.10.2023 08.04	Gorgeous picture indeed
5.	Ronwyn Orchard	24.10.2023 08.46	Yes used to go there in there in my youth. My Sister Rosemary used to work in there.
6.	Rosemary Hunt	24.10.2023 09.35	Remember the juke box, the first in town I believe. Went there just for that, played Lonnie Donegan singing Hang down your head Tom Dooley and Cumberland Gap. Please somebody else remember them too !
7.	Moira Hitchen	24.10.2023 10.41	Rosemary Hunt yeah
8.	Ann Tucker	24.10.2023 15.20	Rosemary Hunt yes remember it well !!
9.	Kate Barden	12.1.2024 14.34	MA Book Everly Brothers Dream, Brian Hyland Sealed with a Kiss.... just talking to my aunty about the cafe and juke box. My aunty lived in St John's House pub (my nan and granddad were the publicans).
10.	Veronica Roni Goff	24.10.2023 10.47	Spent many hours there 1964 onwards blueberry Hill, Dave Clark five, Beatles , Rolling stones and more
11.	Ann Grove	24.10.2023 11.15	Yes, I remember going there. Always thought it was a bit risqué. Don't know why. perhaps because it wasn't the church social club. Who knows.
12.	L Carolyn Jarvis	24.10.2023 11.17	One of the in places of our youth
13.	Marlene Wade	24.10.2023 12.42	Yes
14.	David H T Ninnis	24.10.2023 14.00	My now wife worked there in 1967
15.	Delia O'Donnell	24.10.2023 15.31	I worked there in my holidays I summer of 1963 or 4 .Apache was constantly on the juke box. It was the Riviera Hotel then.
16.	MA Book	26.10.2023 02.07	Delia O'Donnell How was your experience, did you get paid well? Was Mr Dass and good employer?
17.	Delia O'Donnell	26.10.2023 22.46	MA Book I had my wages on time and he paid more than other restaurants. We also had free midday meal I worked in the silver service restaurant at the back under a manageress who dealt with everything so l had little contact with Mr Dass and his family. In the afternoon l worked behind the counter in the cafe I got the job by answering an advert in the Cornishman so no interview involved. Delia O'Donnell Thank you so much. I may want to locate that advert - what year was it please? If you can pinpoint the date - I can go and find the advert. was it 62 or 63? what month too?

18.	Delia O'Donnell	28.10.2023 10.27	MA Book 1963 I think probably June July as it was for summer work. Advert was for Riviera Hotel. Yes right place don't know when photo taken. Why are you writing this book?
19.	David Oats	24.10.2023 19.44	Knew Ronjon well but always found Mac to be pretty sour. The Railway Cafe was part of the town circle every night.
20.	Ali Collins	24.10.2023 22.25	Penny Dass
21.	Abe Harvey	25.10.2023 12.15	Random enquiry on this post
22.	Tony Watson	24.10.2023 22.54	I used to go to school with Robbie Dad's.
23.	M. d. West	9.11.2023 09.12	Link to a book cover I did and loaded on my website.
24.	Jennie Jones	26.10.2023 14.10	Random enquiry on this post
25.	Roger Watson	28.10.2023 00.38	Don't remember it. Pz born (1950) and bred
26.	Mel Mitchell	14.1.2024 19.25	My partner has great memories of hanging out in Maks Bar as a Punk in the early 1982's Loads of his friends went (our first official date took place there....) He said the juke box was great very 80's music and they served a very nice pint of Stella .They were always allowed in as long as they behaved, and generally they did. It was an important social hub for his peers at the time ..... I'm guessing there are a few pictures of them in there around ...amongst our peers ....

MA Book's FB post on "Nostalgic Penzance and Newlyn on 5th November 2023

Thank you **Sylvia Bates** for your support and you got me looking for the Jukebox, so I tracked these down - however, I see they are already listed on your post. I wanted to start a new post - so to target and maybe jog more memories of the **Jukebox** and the pleasure it gave to the youth/young adults of the day. I want to capture some fond memories, positive ones, happy one - this will help to have a balanced content and account of Makhan Lal Dass's life and his contribution to the Penzance community he lived in. I would like to get first hand account of the colour of the "Jukebox" in the cafe? and trhis got 15 comments.

1.	M. d. West	5.11.2023 11.31	Hi...I've deleted all the colour photos of the jukebox I posted so as not to influence anyone's memories of the colour and replaced them with this b&w version I didn't move to Penzance till 1979 so never saw that jukebox, but I lived further up Mount Street from the Makhan Dass family and did visit ' Mak's' bar once or twice around 1983.
2.	Alan Pearce	6.11.2023 08.03	I think I went to school with his son
3.	Sylvia Bates	11.11.2023 00.04	Interesting post from M. d. West.
4.	M. d. West	24.11.2023 20.21	RAF Wireless operator Makhan Lal Dass 1942 Indian Information' magazine article about Makhan Lal Dass joining the RAF A snippet from Indian Information magazine shows up 2nd page of a Google (books field) search for Makhan Lal Dass Indian Information - Volumes 11-12 - Page 109 books.google.co.uk › books 1942 · Snippet view · More editions ... Makhan Lal Dass , a 24 - year - old Indian , is operator at a flying boat station in Scotland . In the interval between sending and receiving messages , he assiduously reads every book on flying that he can lay his hands on ; and , as ... But I got lucky, a fellow on Facebook group Indian Aviation History had scanned the whole article.. don't think there's any more, though. He said he got it from the University of Pennsylvania Library, and Indian Information was a magazine that the Indian embassy in the US put out in WWII
5.	Veronica Roni Goff	25.11.2023 14.42	The one on the right looks familiar bit could have been the one in the Longboat

Glossary Of Terms

A guide to key names, places, and cultural references

Apache - Instrumental hit by The Shadows (1960), frequently mentioned in jukebox memories.

BALAMI E80 - A 1953 British jukebox model remembered for its warm valve sound and distinctive chrome styling.

Blood and Sand - Local band active in the 1960s, part of the wider music scene connected to the café.

Cornishman - Local newspaper that advertised café and Riviera Hotel jobs.

Dass's Café - The family-run café on Market Jew Street that became the centre of youth culture in 1950s–60s Penzance.

Flying-boat station - RAF base in Scotland where Makhan Lal Dass served as a Wireless Operator during WWII.

Hicks Hairdresser's - A landmark next to the café, frequently used in spatial memory.

Indian Information - Government-published magazine (1940s) that profiled Makhan Lal Dass during his RAF service.

Jukebox hacking - A playful trick where teenagers manipulated the table selector to play songs without paying.

Lescudjack School - Secondary school attended by several Dass children and many café regulars.

Mac's Bar - 1980s bar run by Mac Dass, remembered for its jukebox, Stella, and punk-era atmosphere.

Market Jew Street - Main commercial street in Penzance; location of the café.

Mount Street - Location of the first Dass café, run from the family home.

Riviera Hotel - Hotel and restaurant run by the Dass family in the 1960s–70s, known for silver-service dining.

Ronjon & The Trident - Ronjon Dass's first band, active in the 1960s.

The Vandells - Local band featuring Ronjon Dass and other musicians.

Winter Gardens - Popular dance and music venue; part of the café → nightlife circuit.

Note On Sources

How the material in this book was gathered and verified

This book is based primarily on publicly shared community memories posted between 2014 and 2023. These recollections were gathered from:

- local history Facebook groups
- comment threads on historical photographs
- nostalgia pages
- public discussions about Penzance's music and nightlife
- posts relating to the Dass family, the café, and the Riviera Hotel

All material used was publicly visible at the time of collection.

Where possible, memories were cross-checked against:

- multiple independent recollections
- spatial consistency (e.g., WH Smith opposite café)
- known historical facts
- surviving photographs
- newspaper adverts
- RAF documentation
- family testimony

No private messages, restricted content, or unpublished personal data were used.

This book treats memory as a legitimate historical source — subjective, emotional, and deeply human.
Where memories diverged, the book preserves the variation rather than forcing a single narrative.

The goal is not to reconstruct a perfect chronology, but to honour the lived experience of a community.

Final Author's Note

This book began as a simple act of curiosity — a desire to understand how one café, one family, and one generation could leave such a lasting imprint on a town. What emerged was far more than a local history. It became a portrait of belonging, memory, migration, and the quiet power of everyday life.

The Dass story is not mine alone. It belongs to the hundreds of people who shared their recollections, to the family whose presence shaped the social life of Penzance, and to the town that continues to carry these memories forward.

My role has been to listen, to gather, to honour, and to weave these voices into a narrative that reflects their warmth, humour, and humanity.
If this book preserves even a fraction of what Dass's Café meant to those who lived it, then it has done its job.

Thank you for trusting me with your memories.

— *Mayar Akash*